First World War
and Army of Occupation
War Diary
France, Belgium and Germany

42 DIVISION
125 Infantry Brigade
Lancashire Fusiliers
1/7th Battalion
16 June 1916 - 11 April 1919

WO95/2655/1

The Naval & Military Press Ltd
www.nmarchive.com
Published in association with The National Archives

Published by

The Naval & Military Press Ltd

Unit 10 Ridgewood Industrial Park,
Uckfield, East Sussex,
TN22 5QE England
Tel: +44 (0) 1825 749494

www.naval-military-press.com

www.nmarchive.com

This diary has been reprinted in facsimile from the original. Any imperfections are inevitably reproduced and the quality may fall short of modern type and cartographic standards.

© Crown Copyright
Images reproduced by permission of The National Archives, London, England, 2015.

Contents

Document type	Place/Title	Date From	Date To
Heading	WO95/2655/1 1/7 Lancashire Fusiliers-42 Div Mar 1917-Apr 1919		
Heading	42nd Division 125th Infy Bde 1-7th Bn Lancs Fus. Mar 1917-Apr 1919		
Heading	War Diary Of 1/7th Battn Lan. Fus. From March 1st To March 31st 1917 Volume 23		
War Diary	At Sea Marseilles	01/03/1917	02/03/1917
War Diary	On Train	03/03/1917	04/03/1917
War Diary	Bailleul (Abbeville 1/100,000)	05/03/1917	14/03/1917
War Diary	Hamel (Sheet 62 D 1/40,000)	15/03/1917	25/03/1917
War Diary	Eclusier Sheet 62 C 1/40,000	26/03/1917	31/03/1917
Heading	War Diary Of 1/7th Lan. Fus. From April 1-April 30. 1917 Volume 33		
War Diary	Peronne (Ariens 1/100000)	01/04/1917	04/04/1917
War Diary	Tincourt (62.C. NE 1/20,000)	05/04/1917	05/04/1917
War Diary	Longavesnes (62c. NE 1/20,000)	06/04/1917	08/04/1917
War Diary	Epehy (62.c. NE. 1/20,000)	09/04/1917	12/04/1917
War Diary	Epehy	13/04/1917	13/04/1917
War Diary	Longavesnes	14/04/1917	17/04/1917
War Diary	Herbicourt (62c)	18/04/1917	21/04/1917
War Diary	Cartigny (62c)	22/04/1917	30/04/1917
Miscellaneous	Appendix. I		
Operation(al) Order(s)	Appendix I. Operation Order No. 3		
Miscellaneous	Appendix III		
Heading	War Diary Of 1/7th Lancashire Fusiliers May 1st-31st 1917 Vol 4		
War Diary	Cartigny 62C.	01/05/1917	01/05/1917
War Diary	Templeux Le Girard 62c L2	02/05/1917	04/05/1917
War Diary	62c K.5 Central	05/05/1917	09/05/1917
War Diary	Epehy 62c F	10/05/1917	17/05/1917
War Diary	Raisel 62c. K.6	18/05/1917	19/05/1917
War Diary	Villers Faucon 62c E 22	20/05/1917	20/05/1917
War Diary	Equancourt 57c. V.10	21/05/1917	22/05/1917
War Diary	Beaucamp 57c Q12	23/05/1917	25/05/1917
War Diary	Bertincourt 57c. P2	26/05/1917	31/05/1917
Heading	War Diary Of 1/7th Battn Lancashire Fusiliers From June 1st-30th 1917 Volume No. 26		
War Diary	Bertincourt 57c. P2	01/06/1917	05/06/1917
War Diary	Havrincourt Wood 57c. SE	06/06/1917	15/06/1917
War Diary	Havrincourt Wood	16/06/1916	21/06/1916
War Diary	Bertincourt 57c P.7	22/06/1916	30/06/1916
Heading	War Diary Of 1/7 Lan Fus For July 1917 Volume 36		
War Diary	Bertincourt	01/07/1917	05/07/1917
War Diary	Gomiecourt Camp 57c. A28 b.52	06/07/1917	31/07/1917
Heading	War Diary 1/7th Battn Lancashire Fusiliers August 1917 Vol No. 28		
War Diary	Gommiecourt Camp 57c A28 b52	01/08/1917	19/08/1917
War Diary	Bouzincourt	20/08/1917	22/08/1917
War Diary	Mill Camp 27 L. 13.d.44	23/08/1917	28/08/1917
War Diary	Camp. 28. H 17 b.	29/08/1917	31/08/1917

Heading	War Diary Of 1/7 Battn Lancashire Fusiliers. Sept. 1st 30th 1917 Vol. No. 38		
War Diary	Ypres Area. (Sheet 28 NE)	01/09/1917	07/09/1917
War Diary	Toronto Camp 28 NW. G 18a.1.4	08/09/1917	09/09/1917
War Diary	Ypres Area Sheet 28 NE	10/09/1917	18/09/1917
War Diary	Watou Camp 28 NW G 11	19/09/1917	21/09/1917
War Diary	Ledringhem Sheet 27 1 2 b	22/09/1917	23/09/1917
War Diary	Ghyvelde	24/09/1917	25/09/1917
War Diary	St Idesbaldes Sheet 11 SE Wiot	26/09/1917	30/09/1917
Heading	War Diary 1/7 Lan. Fus Oct. 1st-31st 1917 Vol No. 30		
War Diary	St. Idesbald Camp Belgium 11 W 11a 17	01/10/1917	05/10/1917
War Diary	Nieaport Belgium 12 M 28	05/10/1917	21/10/1917
War Diary	Ocst. Dunkerke 11 S.E. 1/20000	22/10/1917	31/10/1917
War Diary	War Diary Of 1/7th Battn. Lancashire Fusiliers Vol No. 40 Nov 1st to Nov. 30th 1917		
War Diary	La Panne Belgium Sheet 11 1/40000	01/11/1917	04/11/1917
War Diary	Nieuport Belgium 12 S.W 1/20000	05/11/1917	18/11/1917
War Diary	Belgium & France Sheet 18 1/40000	19/11/1917	19/11/1917
War Diary	Belgium & France Sheet 27 1/40,000	20/11/1917	22/11/1917
War Diary	France Sheet 36 1/40000	23/11/1917	28/11/1917
War Diary	Guinchy Sheet 36c NW 1/10,000	29/11/1917	30/11/1917
Heading	War Diary Of 1/7th Lan. Fus. 1st 31st December 1917 Volume 41		
War Diary	France 36A 1/40000	01/12/1917	01/12/1917
War Diary	La Bassee 36E N.W. 1/20,000	02/12/1917	03/12/1917
War Diary	France 36B. N.E 1/20000	04/12/1917	08/12/1917
War Diary	France 36A SE 1/20000	09/12/1917	21/12/1917
War Diary	France 36c NW 1/20000	22/12/1917	31/12/1917
Heading	War Diary Of 1/7 Battn Lancashire Fusiliers 1st-31st January 1918 Vol No. 42		
War Diary	France 36c N.W. 1/20000	01/01/1918	09/01/1918
War Diary	France 36B NE 1/20000	10/01/1918	28/01/1918
War Diary	France 36c N.W. 1/20000	29/01/1918	31/01/1918
Heading	War Diary Of 1/7 Battn Lancashire Fusiliers Feb. 1918 Vol 33		
War Diary	France 36B NE. 1: 20000	01/02/1918	07/02/1918
War Diary	France La Bassee 1: 10000	08/02/1918	10/02/1918
War Diary	La Bassee 1: 10000	11/02/1918	14/02/1918
War Diary	France 36B. N.E 1: 20000	14/02/1918	28/02/1918
Heading	42nd Division. 125th Infantry Brigade. 1/7th Battalion Lancashire Fusiliers March 1918		
Heading	War Diary Of 1/7 Batt. Lancs Fus. Vol 44 1st-31st March 1918		
War Diary	France 36B N.E 1: 20000	01/03/1918	15/03/1918
War Diary	France Fouquereil	16/03/1918	31/03/1918
Heading	125th Inf. Bde. 42nd Div. 1/7th Battn. The Lancashire Fusiliers. April 1918		
Heading	War Diary Vol 45 1/7th. Batt. Lancs. Fus. 1-30 April 1918		
War Diary	France Battn. H.Q. Sheet 57 D.E. 29a 8.7	01/04/1918	05/04/1918
War Diary	France Batt. H.Q. Sheet 57.D. F 26 d. 9.6	06/04/1918	08/04/1918
War Diary	Batt H.Q.	09/04/1918	09/04/1918
War Diary	Corps School	10/04/1918	10/04/1918
War Diary	Vauehelles	11/04/1918	11/04/1918
War Diary	France	12/04/1918	16/04/1918
War Diary	Batt. H.Q. K3d 9.9	17/04/1918	21/04/1918

War Diary	France	22/04/1918	28/04/1918
War Diary	Batt. H.Q. J.6.d	29/04/1918	30/04/1918
Heading	War Diary Vol.46 1/7th Battn Lan. Fus. 1-31st May 1918		
War Diary	France Sheet 57D N.E 1.20000 Bn. H.Q. J 6d 3.9 Appendix	01/05/1918	02/05/1918
War Diary	Bn H.Q. K6c 85.65	03/05/1918	04/05/1918
War Diary	Bn. HQ. K6a. 35.45. App.	05/05/1918	06/05/1918
War Diary	Bn H.Q. J 2a. 25.45	07/05/1918	10/05/1918
War Diary	France Sheet 57D N.E. Bn. H.Q. J2a. 25.45	11/05/1918	31/05/1918
Heading	War Diary 1/7th Battn. Lancashire Fusiliers. June 1918 Vol 47		
War Diary	France Ref Sheet 57D N.E Bn. H.Q. J.2a 25.45	01/06/1918	06/06/1918
War Diary	Bn H.Q. J3c. 75.40	07/06/1918	12/06/1918
War Diary	Bn H.Q. J 20.c. 9.4	13/06/1918	13/06/1918
War Diary	France Sheet 57D NE Bn HQ. K9d 10.20	14/06/1918	22/06/1918
War Diary	Bn.H.Q. K 90 60.70	23/06/1918	25/06/1918
War Diary	France Sheet 57d NE Bn HQ K 9a 60.90	26/06/1918	30/06/1918
Heading	War Diary Of 1/7th Bn. Lan. Fus 1st 31st July 1918 Volume 48		
War Diary	France Sheet 57D	01/07/1918	01/07/1918
War Diary	Bn. H.Q. At J 34. L. 2.6	02/07/1918	07/07/1918
War Diary	France Sheet 57D	08/07/1918	09/07/1918
War Diary	Bn. H.Q. At Chalk Pit K 32.a. 2.5	10/07/1918	17/07/1918
War Diary	France Sheet 57D	18/07/1918	24/07/1918
War Diary	Bn H.Q. At J 24 L. 2.6	26/07/1918	26/07/1918
War Diary	France Sheet 57D	26/07/1918	31/07/1918
Heading	War Diary 1/7 Lancashire Fusiliers August 1918 Vol 48		
War Diary	Bertrancourt 57D J33	01/08/1918	02/08/1918
War Diary	J 24b	03/08/1918	10/08/1918
War Diary	K 20 b 1520	11/08/1918	16/08/1918
War Diary	57D J 246	17/08/1918	21/08/1918
War Diary	57d/K 36a 66	22/08/1918	22/08/1918
War Diary	57d/L 25a 93	23/08/1918	23/08/1918
War Diary	K 29d 60 95	24/08/1918	24/08/1918
War Diary	L 34 Central.	25/08/1918	27/08/1918
War Diary	57c/M2b 80	28/08/1918	31/08/1918
War Diary	N/15d 84	31/08/1918	31/08/1918
Heading	War Diary Vol. 30 7th Battn. Lan Fus. 1-30th September 1918 Vol 20		
War Diary	Sheet 57c N.W. B2 H.Q At	01/09/1918	03/09/1918
War Diary	Bn H.Q. At O 15, B 2, 6 Bn. H.Q At O 23d 5.7	04/09/1918	04/09/1918
War Diary	Sheet 57c S.E	05/09/1918	05/09/1918
War Diary	Sheet 57c S.W. Battn. H.Q. At M2d 79	05/09/1918	05/09/1918
War Diary	Sheet 57c S.W	06/09/1918	11/09/1918
War Diary	Sheet 57c S.W Bn. H.Q At M2 D 79	12/09/1918	21/09/1918
War Diary	Sheet 57c NW Bn. H.Q. At I 30a 98	22/09/1918	25/09/1918
War Diary	Batt H.Q. At Q 10b 76	26/09/1918	26/09/1918
War Diary	Sheet 57c S.W	27/09/1918	28/09/1918
War Diary	Battn. H.Q At Q 8a 27	29/09/1918	30/09/1918
Operation(al) Order(s)	Addition No. 1 to 7th. Lan. Fus. Operation Order No. 65	26/09/1918	26/09/1918
Operation(al) Order(s)	7th. Lancashire Fusiliers Operation Order No. 65	29/09/1918	29/09/1918
Operation(al) Order(s)	Table "A" To accompany 7th. Lan. Fus. Operation Order No. 65		

Heading	War Diary Vol 51 7th Battn. Lan. Fus. 1-31 October 1918		
War Diary	France Sheet 5x 55	01/10/1918	01/10/1918
War Diary	Batt H.Q. At Q 8a 8.2	02/10/1918	06/10/1918
War Diary	Sheet 57c SE. Batt. H.Q. At Q. 8a 82	07/10/1918	07/10/1918
War Diary	Batt H.Q. At R 13d 75	08/10/1918	08/10/1918
War Diary	Sheet 57 B 1-40000 Batt H.Q. At N4a 57	09/10/1918	09/10/1918
War Diary	Batt H.Q At I 15c 94 Batt HQ At J 1a 98	10/10/1918	11/10/1918
War Diary	Batt H.Q. At D 26a 83	12/10/1918	12/10/1918
War Diary	Sheet 57b NE Batt. H.Q. At D 26a 93	13/10/1918	14/10/1918
War Diary	Batt. H.Q. At D 28a 51	15/10/1918	17/10/1918
War Diary	Batt H.Q. At I 4c 12	18/10/1918	18/10/1918
Operation(al) Order(s)	Mowe Operatin Order No. 7	22/10/1918	22/10/1918
War Diary	Sheet 57b 1-40000 Batt. H.Q. At D25 b 35	19/10/1918	20/10/1918
War Diary	Batt. H.Q. At E 14a 4.2	21/10/1918	23/10/1918
War Diary	Sheet 57b 1-40000	23/10/1918	23/10/1918
War Diary	Bn. H.Q. At I 15a 71	24/10/1918	25/10/1918
War Diary	Sheet 57b 1-40000	26/10/1918	31/10/1918
Heading	War Diary 7th Lancashire Fusiliers November 1918 Vol 52		
War Diary	France Sheet 57b 1-40000	01/11/1918	01/11/1918
War Diary	Batt H.Q At I 15a 61	02/11/1918	08/11/1918
War Diary	France Sheet 57b 1/4000	08/11/1918	12/11/1918
War Diary	Map Ref. France Sheet 51 1/40000	13/11/1918	30/11/1918
Miscellaneous	Summary Of Operations.	04/11/1918	04/11/1918
Heading	War Diary 7th Lancashire Fusiliers. December 1918 Vol 53		
War Diary	Map Ref. France 51 1/40000	01/12/1918	14/12/1918
War Diary	Sheet 51 1-40000	15/12/1918	21/12/1918
War Diary	France Sheet Namur	22/12/1918	31/12/1918
Miscellaneous	Headquarters. 125. Bde.	01/02/1919	01/02/1919
War Diary	France Sheet Namur 1-100000	01/01/1919	31/01/1919
War Diary	France Belgium Sheet Namur 1-100000	01/02/1919	28/02/1919
Heading	War Diary Vol. 56. 1/7 Batt. Lan. Fus. 1st-31st March. 1919 Vol 26		
War Diary	Belgium Sheet Namur 1-100000	01/03/1919	31/03/1919
War Diary		30/03/1919	30/03/1919
War Diary	Belgium Sheet Namur 1-100000	01/04/1919	11/04/1919

WO95/2655 — 1

1/7 Lancashire Fusiliers — 42 Div

Mar 1917 — Apr 1919

42ND DIVISION
125TH INFY BDE

1-7TH BN LANCS FUS.
MAR 1917 - APR 1919.

CONFIDENTIAL. 175/1

War Diary of 1/7th Battn Lan: Fus:

From

March 1st to March 31st.

1917.

Volume 23.

Army Form C. 2118.

WAR DIARY
or
INTELLIGENCE SUMMARY

(Erase heading not required.)

No. 23, Page 1.

Of 1/7 L.F.
From MARCH 1st – 31st 1918

Instructions regarding War Diaries and Intelligence Summaries are contained in F.S. Regs., Part II. and the Staff Manual respectively. Title pages will be prepared in manuscript.

Place	Date	Hour	Summary of Events and Information	Remarks and references to Appendices
AT SEA	Mar. 1.		Passed ELBA. Swell calm. AMcB	
MARSEILLES	2.		Arrived at MARSEILLES at 0800 entrained ship & entrained at 2030. Left at 2200 with details of 7th Div. H.Q. 126 BZE.M.G. F.A.W.Res. 56 Off. 1269 O.R. AMcB	
ON TRAIN	3.		Passed LYON 1715. AMcB	
	4.		In the train all day. Passed PARIS 2030. Viard. AMcB	
BAILLEUL (ABBEVILLE) (Sheet 60)	5.		Arrived at PONT REMY 0530 marched to BELLIFONTAINE where C.V.D. bags were barrage. V.ORS to BAILLEUL where H.Q. V.A. & B Coys were billeted. 1" of snow. AMcB	
	6.		Drew Transport from ABBEVILLE. 2 cookers, 9 H. draught, 2 B.dgr. mules, 7 Cash mules, 10 G.S. limbers, 4 Cable carriers, 2 W. carts, 1 Mess cart, 1 Maltese cart. AMcB	
	7.		Below nights from PONT REMY (Sheet 60). Coys went on march. AMcB. HqT. SOUTHERN W. joined from ENGLAND. AMcB	
	8.		Coy training. v.cold.	
	9.		Guns still hidden. 8.00 march & box respirators – Coy training AMcB	
	10.		Batt. went march. Received orders to be prepared to move at short notice. AMcB	
	11.		Weather improving. Gas school. Guns warm & sunny. AMcB	
	12.		Strength 36 Off. 922 O.R. Coy training. V.Pct. AMcB	
	13.		Coy training. Orders to move. AMcB	
	14.		Transport left by march route at 0700 for ST. SAUVEUR proceeding on 15th to HAMEL. AMcB	
HAMEL (Sheet 62D) (1/40,000)	15.		Rained to LONGPRE entrained with 5/6 L.F. 1300. Detrained CORBIE & marched to HAMEL arrived 1800 about 15 miles marched altogether on or fell out. AMcB	Ref. Bde. orders Nos 1 & 2
	16.		Bn. visited Coy inspection & parades. Bath billeted in huts. AMcB	
	17.		Draft to ENGLAND cancelled. Coy parades. AMcB. Silence pass rejoined from trenches. AMcB	
	18.		Parade service. New platoon formation practised. AMcB. Capt. KELLY proceeded for instruction to 1st Bn trenches for 2 days. AMcB	
	19.		Coy parade. AMcB	
	20.		" " Col. MASKELL proceeded to ENGLAND on leave. Capt. SAUNDERS to 1st Bn trenches. AMcB	
	21.		Batt. marched to Camp No.60 about 2 kilos from HAMEL. Coy training in the late morning & afternoon. V.cold. AMcB	
	22.		Coys started digging for trenches – V.cold – Snowing. 20th DECCAN HORSE & 7th II.G. & POONA HORSE came into our camp & occupied left of L.F. AMcB	
	23.		Batt. filled with Box respirators & went through gas chamber. Coy training. AMcB	

WAR DIARY of 1/7 L.F.

or

INTELLIGENCE SUMMARY. From MARCH 1st, 1918.

Vol 23 Page 2

Army Form C. 2118.

Place	Date 1917	Hour	Summary of Events and Information	Remarks and references to Appendices
HAMEL Sheet 62d 1/40,000	Mar 24.		The enemy left at 8.00 AM. A, B, & D. Coy had hot baths at BOUZENCOURT. A/H.B	Ref 13-Batt Orders No 3.
	25.		Marched at 7.40 & proceeded by route march to ECLUSIER - good road, 3 falls out, arrived about 2.45 P.m. & took over a camp (huts) & dirty. Tents expected. A/H.B	
ECLUSIER Sheet 62c 1/40,000	26.		Foot Inspection. Cleaned camp & making foot paths good. B Coy paraded in the afternoon in active V.act. A/H.B	
	27.		LT. J. SWINDELLS reported for duty. B Coy paraded. A v B Coy finding working party 300 O.R. in during March at FLAUCOURT. A/H.B	
	28.		Working Parties. 200 to BARLEUX, 200 to HERBECOURT. A/H.B	
	29.		" 300 " FLAUCOURT. C Coy parades for rest of Batt. A/H.B	
	30.		" 200 " BARLEUX, 200 to HERBECOURT. A/H.B	
	31.		Batt. moved by route march to PERONNE 9.00 A.M. Strength 38 off. 861 O.R. A/H.B	

22.L.
9 sheets

Vol 3

Confidential

WAR DIARY

OF

1/5th LAN. FUS.

From April 1 — April 30, 1917

Volume 33

Army Form C. 2118.

WAR DIARY of 1/7th Lan Fus
or
INTELLIGENCE SUMMARY.
(Erase heading not required.)

Place	Date 1917	Hour	Summary of Events and Information	Remarks and references to Appendices
PERONNE (Amiens 10000)	APR 1		Parties engaged repairing roads. PKS	
	2		Parties engaged repairing roads. Capt. P.E. BRIERLEY adjutant rejoined from hospital in EGYPT. Lt. P.A. SHELMERDINE rejoined after 5 weeks leave at home. PKS At 8pm orders	
	3		Parties engaged repairing roads. Lt. Major CADE & Capt. E.M. AVENELL rejoined at 5 weeks leave. received to move to TINCOURT. PKS	
TINCOURT (L6C. NE 20000)	4	4.15 AM	Capt PERONNE arrived TINCOURT. 7.0 AM. Reported to 98 Div. H.Q. and were billetted. Later received orders and moved to LONGAVESNES where we again billetted. PKS	
LONGAVESNES (L6C. NE 20000)	6		Parties of 400 men road mending. PKS	
	7		Parties of 400 men road mending. A on right B on left. see Appendix I	
	8		Moved to EPEHY and relieved 1/7 ROYAL WARWICKS. A and B coys in main defence. Trenches were C coy found 1 platoon as outpost in TETARD WOOD (37 E 20) . D coy in reserve. improved and wiring continued. PKS	
EPEHY (b2C. NE 20000)	9		Quiet day. After dark 1 Platoon of A coy under 2/Lt. Buckley relieved 1 platoon of 1/8 WORCESTERS in MALASSISE FARM. (b2 F 8 b) where by day the men live in a big cellar, and by night manned the trenches One platoon of C coy relieved A coy's left platoon. 5/LF relieved 1m on our left and left. GLOUCESTER'S relieved by us on our right. PKS	
	10		In evening enemy heavily shelled TETARD WOOD where 2 men were killed and 1 wounded. The remains of the front was quiet. PKS The FARM was shelled intermittently all day.	
	11		Quiet day. Except for MALASSISE FARM which was shelled. After dark 2/Lt ANDEXSER recommoitred NO NAME COPSE X.27 c 7.4 with 6 men which will LT BUCKLEY with a (Map 57C SE) which he reported not held by enemy. He met patrol killing 1 man. Small party recommoitred No. B COPSE which within 200 yds became under rifle fire having 1 man wounded. Snow on the ground made secrecy impossible. PKS (Capt AVENELL to LoftY) Casualties and held our own. see appendix II	
	12		Very quiet day. At 9 pm we advanced our outpost, dug trenches Casualties Lt SWINDELLS appendix III position being relieved by 6/LF (1 coy) in advance post. C/LF were attacked as wounded. Ors 1 killed 1 dies of wounds 6 wounded. PKS	

WAR DIARY of 17th Jan Fus

INTELLIGENCE SUMMARY

Army Form C. 2118.

Place	Date 1917	Hour	Summary of Events and Information	Remarks and references to Appendices
EPEHY	Apr. 13		Enemy heavily shelled N'th COPSE and MALASSISE FARM. Colley, at farm was blown in with aerial casualties. Total casualties 1 killed, 5 wounded. 6LF 2 Coys attacked 2 Killed 10 wounded, 2 shell shock chiefly at farm. Relieved at night by remainder 6LF and 1 Coy 8LF. Marched back to relieve to LONGAVESNES. P.K.S	
LONGAVESNES	14		Rest for all ranks. Clean clothing issued for all men. P.K.S	
	15		Parties out road repairing at VILLERS FAUCON and SAULCOURT (6½ N.E) P.K.S	
	16		As yesterday. P.K.S	
	17		Left LONGAVESNES 9.0am and marched to FLAUCOURT. Billeted in dugouts near FLAUCOURT. Dugouts were very damp. P.K.S	
HERBECOURT (6c)	18		Bn. H.q. and A Coy moved to HERBECOURT. B.C. and D Coys to FLAUCOURT. P.K.S	
	19		Small fatigue parties engaged repairing roads; the remainder training under Coy arrangements. P.K.S	
	20		Same as yesterday. P.K.S	
	21		100 men A Coy moved to BRIE (Map 6C), C Coy moved to MESNIL-BRUNTEL (6C) Bn. Hq. and remainder moved to CARTIGNY. P.K.S	
CARTIGNY (6c)	22		All available men engaged on road repairing. Capt W Kelly takes up duties of Supervising officer 43 Div Detail Camp PERONNE ? Lt Weyman of Town Major at CAPPY. P.K.S	
	23		As yesterday. P.K.S	
	24		As yesterday. Lt Kershaw to hospital. P.K.S	
	25		As yesterday. Remainder of A Coy and 1 Platoon C Coy moved to BRIE. Lt Spink Yeoman posted to Pont Remy musketry Course. P.K.S	
	26		As yesterday. D Coy moved to PERONNE. P.K.S	
	27		As yesterday. 1 Platoon B Coy moved to PERONNE. P.K.S	
	28		As yesterday. P.K.S	
	29		As yesterday. A Coy at BRIE ordered to be prepared to rejoin Bn. tomorrow. P.K.S	
	30		As yesterday. Total strength of Bn. 35 officers 1784 or. Less Coys now BRIE and PERONNE minus PERONNE minus. P.K.S	

F.M. Hill Lt Col
Commd. 17 Lan Fus.

Appendix I.
Page 8.   Refce maps 57C.SE. & 62C.NE
Hamlin

B Coy. from station 57C SE X25c90 to Cemetery. 62C NE F1b57 in front of railway embankment. This Consisted of a series of trenches about 20yds apart with Lewis gun emplacements which we were wiring and which would eventually be linked up into a continuous trench.

A Coy. from 62C F1b66 to F2c25. A series of 4 trenches in front of Ry. embankment. These trenches were held at night and in day time troops were withdrawn to railway embankment.
Listening posts were dug and manned by night

Tetard wood was an outpost held by 1 platoon of C coy which was relieved each night. There were also 2 Lewis guns.

PTB

Secret.　　　　Copy

Appendix I Operation Order.　　　No 3
　Map reference　57 C.SE and 62C NE

<u>1</u> The outpost line on the battⁿ front will be advanced tonight on the line RED RUIN X 27 a 41 to N°12 COPSE F36.

<u>2</u> One platoon D coy under 2Lt ANDERSER will leave TETARD WOOD at zero and proceed to occupy NO NAME COPSE X27c 7.6 and RED RUIN X27a 41. One platoon of 6 LF will follow in support and will help to establish positions on new line.

<u>3</u> One platoon D coy will leave MALASSISE FARM at zero, and proceed to occupy N° 12 Copse.
One platoon D coy. will follow in support and one platoon D Coy will remain in the FARM as local reserve — The whole of the party under Capt. KELLY.
The leading platoon will take the copse by storm if occupied by the enemy.

and will endeavour to cut off and capture the enemy. The supports will come up & dig in positions on the new line for one platoon.

4 When the new positions are established the D Coy platoons will withdraw from the new positions leaving one platoon 6th LF between the post near RED RUIN and NO NAME COPSE. One platoon 6LF will also relieve one platoon A coy in MALASSISE FARM.

5 2000 will be 9 pm for all objectives

6 The supports will bring up sufficient tools to quickly establish the new positions.

7 Care must be taken to screen our positions by from observation by day as much as possible

8 Our artillery will fire upon our objectives until Zero +15 when it

Appendix III

2/Lt. ANDEXSER advanced from TETARD WOOD and occupied UNNAMED FARM 57c 27c.7.6 and RUINED HOUSE 57c 27a 4.1. He occupied each with half a platoon without opposition and when consolidated was relieved by 1 platoon 6.LF.

Lt SWINDELLS lead the fighting platoon with Capt KELLY in support 100 yds in rear. The supports lost touch and returned to the farm, meanwhile Lt. SWINDELLS attacked and was met by rifle fire. He got through the wood to find a party of the enemy coming round in the rear. He therefore withdrew and found the supports at the farm, reorganising. Lt SWINDELLS was wounded.
Capt KELLY with 2 platoons again went up to the copse and occupied it this time without opposition. He dug in and was relieved by 6LF.

will lift to enable the final assaults to be made

9. When positions have been taken up a telephone line will be run out to No. 12 COPSE. Frequent reports should be sent in to Battn. Hd Qrs. as to situation.

10. Fighting troops should be kept apart from working troops as far as possible

Issued at 6 pm.
  to OC D Coy. 1 copy
     Lt Anderson 1 .
     OC B/125 1 .
     File 1 .

       Signed. A. DEBENHAM
                     capt & adj
                       1/7. Lan. Fus

CONFIDENTIAL.

Vol 4

WAR DIARY
of
1/7th LANCASHIRE FUSILIERS

May 1st – 31st
1917

23.2.
3 sheets
Marsh

Vol. No. 34.

Army Form C. 2118.

WAR DIARY of 2/7th LAN FUS

or

INTELLIGENCE SUMMARY.

(Erase heading not required.)

Instructions regarding War Diaries and Intelligence Summaries are contained in F. S. Regs., Part II. and the Staff Manual respectively. Title pages will be prepared in manuscript.

Place	Date 1917	Hour	Summary of Events and Information	Remarks and references to Appendices
CARTIGNY. b.c.	May 1		Left CARTIGNY and marched to ROISEL, arriving midday. At 4 pm left ROISEL to relieve 7th WORCESTERS. Barn in support to 5LF. Hqrs and A Coy Eye Wd. B Coy iT TOMBE WOOD F.38.b. C and D Coy in rear of hu.by. C & D Coy on digging fatigue at night making communication trench from GUILLEMONT FARM (U.3. Area) H.R.M. ARCHER and 2 O.R. killed while working. 2 O.R. wounded.	PF3
TEMPLEUX LE GUIRARD 28.c.4	2		Whole bn digging at night except B Coy who manned known line of defence in case of alarm.	PF3
	3		C and D Coy on fatigue and working parties at night.	PF3
	4		Bn relieved at 7.0 pm by 4th EAST LANCS. Went back to rest camp in K5 central as divisional reserve.	PF3
K5 Central	5		A Coy Coy to LEMPIRE, B Coy to TOMBE WOOD to take known line	PF3
	6		A & B Coy supply working parties. C and D Company training.	PF3
	7		C Coy relieves B. D Coy relieves A.	PF3
	8		C and D supply working parties in known line. A & B Company training.	PF3
	9		Relieved 5th MANCHESTERS in front line, in rt. half of div left sector.	PF3
EPEHY b.c.f.	10		A Coy in outpost line. B Coy & D in main line of resistance. B Coy Hq near CATELET COPSE (57.c X.2.8) D recon PRIEL FARM (b.c & F.4.b.) C Coy in reserve. Quiet day. Trenches improved. One of our aeroplanes brought down near CATELET COPSE. 8LF in sight of hn.	PF3
	11		Quiet day. Working parties at night.	PF3
	12		Very quiet day. Working parties at day.	PF3
	13		Relieved by 6LF and came back in support, all bn in Epehy. D Coy making outer remainder in cellars &c. No casualties.	PF3
	14		Hqrs and working parties at night.	PF3
	15		Whole bn employed difficult communication trench to outpost line at night. Strength of bn 35 officers 770 or. bn with later 32 officers 543 other ranks.	PF3

WAR DIARY or INTELLIGENCE SUMMARY

Army Form C. 2118

of 1/7th Lan. Fus.

Place	Date 1917	Hour	Summary of Events and Information	Remarks and references to Appendices
EREHY 62c K.7.	May 16		Whole Bn. on fatigue at night, also wiring parties. PJB	
	17		Relieved by 16th LANCERS 2nd Dismounted Division, marched to Camp K.12.c PJB	
ROISEL 62c K.13	18		Coy. inspections &c. PJB	
	19		Left Camp and marched to VILLERS FAUCON, billetted for night. PJB	
VILLERS FAUCON 62c E.21 EQUANCOURT 57c V.10	20		Left VILLERS FAUCON 13.30. 3rd Bn. in the column of route, and marched to EQUANCOURT. Took over billets of 4th B.L. A very hot day. PJB	
	21		Coy training. PJB	
BEAUCAMP 57c Q.3	22		Took over front line from KRR. BCD Coys in firing line which was a continuous trench. 4 Blow left 5 LF on right. Bn hq in dunken road from BEAUCAMP to VILLERS PLOUICH. Line about ½ mile in front of bn hq. 57c R.19 PJB	
	23		Quiet day. Trenches improved and drained. PJB	
	24		Quiet day. Work as yesterday. PJB	
	25		Relieved by 6 LF. During relief heavy enemy barrage on the right of our front. 2 men wounded while on working party. PJB	
BERTINCOURT 57c P.2	26		Arrived BERTINCOURT. Batto. billetted in village. Also 8 LF. Lt ANDERSON to hospital. PJB 57c P.2	
	27		Coy training. PJB	
	28		150 men on fatigue, remainder training. PJB	
	29		200 men on fatigue, remainder training. Lt THORP C.D. joins bn from ENGLAND. PJB	
	30		100 men on fatigue, remainder training. G.O.C. 125 I.B. inspected bn. transport. PJB	
	31		200 men on fatigue. PJB Strength bn. 34 officers 786 o.r. with batts. 20 officers & 554 o.r. PJB	

Confidential

Vol 5

24.L
3 sheets

WAR DIARY
of
1/7th Battn Lancashire Fusiliers
from June 1st - 30th.
1917.

VOLUME No. 26.

WAR DIARY of 1/7 Lan Fus
or
INTELLIGENCE SUMMARY

Army Form C. 2118

Place	Date 1917	Hour	Summary of Events and Information	Remarks and references to Appendices
BERTINCOURT 57c F.2	June 1		GOC inspected bn in transport lay. Private in afternoon. PXS	
	2		Working parties found for R.E's. PXS	
	3		2Lt A.F.Leigh rejoined bn from ENGLAND. Working parties found for R.E's. PXS	
	4		Working parties found as yesterday. PXS	
	5		Relieved 9th MANCHESTERS in front line. Hqr at Q14b.44. D coy at a point 200yds in front in front line. A and B coys in front line from right Bow reserve. C coy in support hqr at Q10a.55. Trench from Q5a.50 to Q9a.61. 3 posts in front at Q4b.57. PXS. left. Trench from Q10a.55 to Q9a.61. Communication trench to & towards pot Q4b.57 dug through and deepened.	
LAURINCOURT WOOD 57c SE	6		Quiet day. Trenches improved. PXS	
	7		Others & DERBY on right. 5LF on left. PXS. Very quiet day. Heavy thunderstorm in afternoon made trenches very wet. Digging continued at night. PXS	
	8		Very quiet day. Digging continued at night. PXS	
	9		Very quiet. Digging and wiring at night. PXS	
	10		A coy close up to right. B coy to left. C coy move in between. D coy from reserve move up to C coys old position. PXS.	
	11		Bn relieved by 5LF. Working parties found for front line immediately on relief. After relief bn hqr move to P.18b.61. 2 coys near and running N&S in Quy. 2 coys near road running NW-SE in Q8. 3 Q15. PXS	
	12		Relieved by 9 BWFus, and in turn relieved 6LF. Hq & B&C coys at Q7b.75.15. PXS. Working parties found for front line at night. Bn killed 7, wounded while in line PXS.	
	13		Same as yesterday. PXS.	
	14		Strength of bn 37 others 774 or. with bn 24 others 590 or. left Bn in centre of bde line, next sector north of previous line. Relieved 2LF in front line. Bn in centre of bde line, next sector north of previous line. 5LF on right. 6LF on [left]. D coy on right. C in centre. A on right. B in support.	
	15		MG and trench mortar activity at night. Bn hqr at Q8d.07. PXS	

WAR DIARY of 1/7 LAN Fus

or

INTELLIGENCE SUMMARY

(Erase heading not required.)

Army Form C. 2118

Instructions regarding War Diaries and Intelligence Summaries are contained in F. S. Regs., Part II. and the Staff Manual respectively. Title Pages will be prepared in manuscript.

Place	Date 1916	Hour	Summary of Events and Information	Remarks and references to Appendices
HAVRINCOURT WOOD	June 16		Bn. hq. moved to advance hq. at Q3d14. Orderly room remaining told hq. New hq. a deep dugout in a small quarry. At night trenches improved and wired. Trenches improved in day also for the Bn right. Usual activity of enemy trench mortars and machine guns. PAS	
	17		Work continued as yesterday. Usual enemy activity at night PAS	
	18		Heavy rain made trenches very muddy. Enemy quiet at night. Work continued. PAS	
	19		Lt. PEAKE wounded. Occasional thunderstorms make trenches very bad. Work continued and Major CADE wounded by remaining in line Make pumps out of trenches. Enemy more active than usual with artillery PAS	
	20		More rain. About 1 foot mud in communication trenches. Enemy shelling during evening Quiet night. Work continued. PAS	
	21		Relieved by 1/5 Man and marched to old headquarters. Total casualties while in line Address is Ba or. Bes (Akid Browned knowing) PAS	
PERTINCOURT S/EP7.	22		By light railway to STRET-BERTINCOURT ROAD. Then marched to ots billet at BERTINCOURT. Men have bath at Div. baths during day. PAS	
	23		Working party of officer 40 or for TOWN MAJOR. Coy Parade for remainder. PAS	
	24		Coy parade. PAS	
	25		Route march for Bn and march past GOC 125 Bde. PAS	
	26		Inspection by GOC 125 Bde. PAS	
	27		Bn. attend Div. Gas school in morning by coys. Coy Parades in afternoon. PAS	
	28		Coy parade. Range firing for A.B.C. coys. PAS	
	29		Range firing for Dcoy & details. Working parties found for REs. PAS	
	30		Range firing for B. Coy. Groups of two Brothers 7/7 Lt. with two 2d officers 6.15 +s. PAS Working party found for RES.	

Vol 6 175/42

25.L
4 sheets

CONFIDENTIAL

War Diary
of
1/7 Sam Fus
July 1917

Volume 36

Army Form C. 2118

WAR DIARY of 1/7 Lan Fus
or
INTELLIGENCE SUMMARY
(Erase heading not required.)

Instructions regarding War Diaries and Intelligence Summaries are contained in F. S. Regs., Part II. and the Staff Manual respectively. Title Pages will be prepared in manuscript.

Place	Date	Hour	Summary of Events and Information	Remarks and references to Appendices
BERTINCOURT	July 1		1 Coy on R.E. fatigue in BERTINCOURT. Coy training for remainder. PAS	
	2		As yesterday. PAS	
	3		As yesterday. PAS	
	4		As yesterday. PAS	
	5		As yesterday in morning. Bn marched to YTRES for the sports in afternoon. PAS	
GOMIECOURT Camp Sqr A28 B52	6		Left BERTINCOURT 5.30 AM. Marched to camp Sqr. A28 B52 nr. GOMIECOURT, (via BUS, ROCQUIGNY, LE TRANSLOY and BAPAUME). In VI Corps III Army reserve. PAS	
	7		Camp cleaned and repaired. CO's inspection. PAS	
	8		Very heavy thunderstorm in night, rain continued all morning. Church Parade cancelled. PAS	
	9		Coy training. Bertinhill, Lewis gun, bombs etc. Hours 7.15-7.45 AM. 9.0 to 1 PM. 2.30-4.0 PM. PAS	
	10		Coy training as yesterday. PAS	
	11		Coy training as yesterday. PAS	
	12		Route march 9-1 pm. PAS	
	13		Coy parades as on 9th. PAS	
	14		Coy parades as yesterday. PAS	
	15		Coy parades in morning. PAS	
	16		Coy parades in morning. Strength of Bn. 34 officers 763 ors. with 1 or. 27 other 629 ors. PAS	
	17		Church parade 10.30 am. PAS	
	18		Coy parades, bayonet fighting, platoon drill, Lewis guns bombers etc. Hoo 13 & 101 week. PAS	
	19		Coy parades as yesterday. Coys in turn practice attack in new formation. PAS	
	20		Coy parades as yesterday. 9 am to 1 pm. PAS	
	21		Bn route march 9 am to 17h. PAS	
	22		Coy parades as on 17th. PAS	
	23		Coy parade as yesterday. Lecture to Bn. at 11.15 by Bn Bayonet fighting 5 pm. PAS	
	24		Coy parades as yesterday. PAS	
	25		Coy parades in morning. PAS	
	26		Bde. Church parade 10.0 AM. Afterwards march past GOC 42nd Division. PAS	

WAR DIARY of 1/7½ Lan. Fus.
INTELLIGENCE SUMMARY

Army Form C. 2118

Place	Date 1917	Hour	Summary of Events and Information	Remarks and references to Appendices
AINTREE COURT CAMP Ex Area/51	July 23		Coy parades. Coy drill. Bombers learn from bayonet fighting. Pans twigs in last week. PAS	
	24		Coy parades as yesterday. PAS	
	25		Bn route march 8 am to 2 pm. 2 Lt. W. Steele joined bn. PAS	
	26		Coy parades as 23rd. PAS	
	27		Coy parades as yesterday. PAS	
	28		Coy parades in morning. PAS	
	29		Church parade 9.0 am. Bde ceremonial drill to be held afternoon cancelled owing to rain. PAS	
	30		2 Lt JM Whyte to hospital. Draft of 28 men joined bn. PAS 2 Lt G.A. Green joined bn. Bath parties. "no-unifrom"afternoon in attack with aeroplane contact. PAS	
	31		In morning battalion in attack with aeroplane contact for GOC 55 bde's inspection. PAS Bde ceremonial drill in afternoon. PAS Strength of bn. 36 officers 791 ors. withdrew. 22 officers 6230 ors. PAS	

Signed Major
Commanding
1/7 Lan. Fus.

CONFIDENTIAL.

WAR DIARY

17th Battn Lancashire Fusiliers.

August 1917.

Vor: No: 98

Army Form C. 2118.

WAR DIARY of 1/7th Lancs. Fus.
or
INTELLIGENCE SUMMARY.
(Erase heading not required.)

Instructions regarding War Diaries and Intelligence Summaries are contained in F.S. Regs., Part II. and the Staff Manual respectively. Title pages will be prepared in manuscript.

Place	Date	Hour	Summary of Events and Information	Remarks and references to Appendices
GOMMIECOURT CAMP 57cA19 b52	Aug 1		Heavy Thunderstorm during night, rain continued in morning. Inspection by G.O.C. 42nd Div. cancelled. AAA	
	2		Bn. Company firing on range. Remainder Coy Training, Bombing, Bayonet fighting, Lewis Gun, Physical Training. AAA	
	3	7.Iv - 7.45am. 9.0am - 1.0pm. 2.30 - 4.30pm	Coy Training. 2.30pm - 4.0pm. Draft of 88 men joined Battn. AAA	
		Hours 7.15 - 8.15am	Battn. Attack Practice. 10.0 - 1.0pm. Coy Training. 2.30pm - 4.0pm. Draft of 88 men	
		9.0am	Batt. Notification received of 3 D.C.M's awarded for GALLIPOLI CAMPAIGN. AAA	
	4	7.30 - 1.30pm	Bde. Route March. AAA	
	5	9.0am	Batt. Church Parade Served. AAA	
	6		Battn. Field Firing in LOUPART WOOD morning and afternoon. AAA	
	7		Coy Parades as on 2nd. AAA	
	8		Bn. Route March 9.0am - 1.0pm. Compulsory Games 2.30pm - 6.0pm AAA	
	9		Coy Parade as on 2nd. Cos in turn do Company attack Practice. Draft of 88 men joined Battn. AAA	
	10		Coy Parades as yesterday. AAA	
	11	9.0am - 10.0am	Battn. Drill. Coy Training as yesterday. AAA	
	12	9.0am	Bde Church Parade Served. 9.0am. Drafts of 50 men joined Bn. AAA	
	13		Coy Parades as on 8th. AAA	
	14		As yesterday. AAA	
	15		As yesterday in morning. Sports in afternoon Draft of 70 men joined Bn. AAA	
	16		Two companies firing on Range. Remainder of Bn. Coy attack Practice.	
			Strength of Bn. 36 off. 963 OR. W.H. R. 22 off. 805 OR. AAA	
	17		Battn. Attack Practice 9.0am - 4.0pm AAA	
	18		Coy attack Practice 9.0am - 4.0pm. AAA	
	19	10.0am	Church Parade 10.0am AAA	
BOUZINCOURT	20	9.0am	Left GOMMIECOURT 9.0am marched to BOUZINCOURT (via ACHET-LE-PETIT—MIRAUMONT—BEAUCOURT—MESNIL—MARTINSART—BOUZINCOURT) Billeted there. AAA	
	21		C.O's Inspection in morning. Swimming up drill in afternoon. AAA	
	22		Coy Inspections and something up drill. Lt. Col. BOUZINCOURT at 6.0pm	
		9.0pm	Bn. at 9.0pm. MAJOR J.S. KNYVETT, 1st WARWICK'S joined Battn. as 2nd. in Command. AAA	
	23		Arrived at GODEWAERSVELDE. Detrained Here and marched to ALBERT. Entrained up drill. HILL CAMP (27 L.13.a.44). AAA	
	24		Coy Parades. Organizing Platoons and examining up drill. AAA	
	25		Coy and Platoon attack Schemes in morning. Coy Training in afternoon. AAA	
	26	11.0am	Church Parade 11.0am. 12.0 - 1.0pm. Battn. Ceremonial Parade AAA	
MILL CAMP. 27 L.13.d.H.H.	27		Coy and Platoon attack Schemes in morning. Coy Training in afternoon. AAA	

(A7092). Wt. W12859/M1293. 750,000. 1/17. D.D. & L., Ltd. Forms/C.2118/14.

WAR DIARY
or
INTELLIGENCE SUMMARY.
(Erase heading not required.)

Army Form C. 2118.

Place	Date	Hour	Summary of Events and Information	Remarks and references to Appendices
MILL CAMP 27 L.12.a.44.	Aug.28.		Coy. and Platoon Attack Practice in morning. Coy. Training in afternoon. B/HQ.	
CAMP. 28.H.17.b.	" 29		Left MILL CAMP 11.0 a.m., marched to POPERINGE. Entrained here. Detrained at YPRES. Marched to Camp 28.H.17.b. B/HQ.	Map references on sheet 28.
	" 30		Coy. inspections in morning. Left Camp 28.H.17.b. at 8 p.m. Relieved 7th 6/7 R.SCOTS FUSILIERS. We occupied IBEX RESERVE TRENCH ("A" and "B" Coys.) I.6.a.37 to I.6.c.98. IBEX SUPPORT TRENCH ("C" Coy.) I.5.b.65 to I.6.a.20 and O.B.1 ("D" Coy.) I.5.a.38 to I.5.d.b5. Considerable artillery activity. B/HQ.	
	" 31		Considerable artillery activity. Casualties 1 O.R. killed 4 O.R. wounded. 2nd Lt. GREEN. G.A. slightly wounded (at duty). Considerable aerial activity. Strength B Bn. 36 off. 932 O.R. With Bn. 24 off. 756 O.R. B/HQ.	

M. Maxwell
Lt.Col.
Commanding B/Shere Divn.

Confidential

WAR DIARY
of
1/7 Batt. LANCASHIRE FUSILIERS.

Sep 1st - 30th 1917

Vol. No. 38

Army Form C. 2118.

WAR DIARY of 1/7th Bon 7w
or
INTELLIGENCE SUMMARY.
(Erase heading not required.)

Vol No 38:

Instructions regarding War Diaries and Intelligence Summaries are contained in F. S. Regs, Part II. and the Staff Manual respectively. Title pages will be prepared in manuscript.

Place	Date 9/17	Hour	Summary of Events and Information	Remarks and references to Appendices
YPRES AREA (Sheet 28 NE)	Sept. 1		Considerable aerial & artillery activity throughout the day. Attempt to back up positions in front line relieving 5LF. 2nd Lt. C&D occupied firing line D5a 8.7 to D5o.B7 A&B in local support. PAS	
	2		Relief completed 1.30am. Considerable artillery activity. Carpenters actively shelled. Intermovement of trench carried out. Communication to Camp were temporarily broken several times. Casualties 9 wounded. PAS	
	3		Artillery of both sides very active both day & night. A considerable number of gas shells fired in rear of our position. 3 prisoners captured in our line. Casualties 2 killed 3 wounded. PAS	
	4		Continuous aerial activity and artillery fire all morning. Fairly quiet afternoon till 7.30pm when our guns opened a heavy fire. Casualties 2 wounded. PAS	
	5		Relieved by 5LF. Enemy artillery fired all day, also a large number of gas shells in evening. Casualties 1 Killed 4 wounded. 2/Lt. HEATON 4 wounded. PAS	
	6		4.30am Barrage and bombardment of enemy lines. 5LF (6LF attacked) objectives being IBERIAN, (D19/32), PECK HOUSE, SPAN, BORRY FARM, D5+7/2, a left in support of 5LF. Enemy counter attack was unsuccessful. Casualties 4 killed 26 wounded. PAS	
	7		Enemy artillery quieter. Trenches improved and repaired. Relieved by 7th MANCHESTERS, commenced at 10.30pm Casualties 7 wounded 1 missing. PAS	
TORONTO CAMP 28NW.G18 I.14	8		Relief completed 1.30am. Marched to Asylum YPRES, and entrained. Detrained at BRANDHOEK, marched to TORONTO CAMP arriving 3am. CO's inspection in afternoon. PAS (28NW. G9.a.1.4)	
YPRES AREA Sheet 28 NE.	9		Inspection in morning. Left camp 7.30pm. & proceeded by busses to YPRES. Relieved 6th MANCHESTERS in left support C+D in OG3 C5q.a 8.9 to C5q.d 9.51 A+B Camp in OG1. D5q.A 5.7 to D5q.d 5.2 Both artilleries very active. Casualties 2 wounded. PAS	
	10		Relief completed 11.0am. Trenches improved & repaired during day. Carrying parties to firing line supplies at night. Casualties 13 wounded. PAS	
	11		Artillery of both sides active. Works continued on trenches. Casualties 1 Killed 7 wounded. 2/Lt CRAMPTON & Lt SCHOFIELD sick to hospital. PAS Lt CA GREEN.	

Army Form C. 2118.

WAR DIARY
or
INTELLIGENCE SUMMARY.
(Erase heading not required.)

of 1/4th Lan. Fus.

Instructions regarding War Diaries and Intelligence Summaries are contained in F. S. Regs., Part II and the Staff Manual respectively. Title pages will be prepared in manuscript.

Place	Date 1917	Hour	Summary of Events and Information	Remarks and references to Appendices
YPRES area (Oost Dene)	Sept 12		Artillery activity considerable. Trenches repaired. 10.30pm relieved by 6th MANCHESTERS. Lt A Buckley to hospital. Marched to YPRES ASYLUM and entrained arriving TORONTO camp 4.0 a.m.	PR3
	13		Lt Col G.P. Brewis TRENWELCH REGT took over command vice Lt Col WE MASKELL	PR3
	14		Lt Col WE MASKELL proceeded to leave. Impractical in morning (left camp 7.30 p.m. and proceeded by train to YPRES. Then took over line A, C + D Coy in line (Reinforced by two 5th Manchesters) A + B in support. Casualties 3 wounded.	PR3
	15		Trenches improved & repaired. Heavy Artillery fire all day. Casualties 2 wounded. Strength 35 officers 890 or with battn. 20 others 63 or	PR3
	16		Work carried on in trenches, which were shelled all day at intervals.	PR3
	17		A patrol went out and ascertained no enemy at 6.30 a.m. starving at 1.30 a.m. Very little enemy activity to our Considerable bombardment.	PR3
	18		Relieved by 3/ S.A. I.T. and arrived at Camp 2A.M. Breakfast 5.0 a.m	PR3
WATON Camp 28th Div Guest	19		Left Camp & marched to a Camp at WATON.	PR3
	20		Parade for all in morning. Parade 2.15 to 4 p.m. Lt FA MAINPRICE + Lt LM MORRISON (Liverpool) attached to he acting Captains.	PR3
	21		Training for bn. 9-12 AM. 2-3 pm	PR3
LEDRINGHEM Sept 22 1st GUYELDE	22 23 24		Entrained at HOPOUTRE Sidings 10.30 am. arrived ARNEKE. Bn Whites in area round LEDRINGHEM. Co's Paraded r Church Parade. Marched to ESQUELBERG 7.55 am. and entrained arrived GUYVELDE and marched to camp. Bn Attached 186 JCB	PR3 PR3 PR3
GUYVELDE	25		Left GUYVELDE 1pm and marched to Camp at STDESBALD	PR3
ST DESBALD 1st Division	26		A. B. C Coys attached to 184 Tunnelling Coy RE for fatigues, and proceeded by road to COTYDE	PR3

WAR DIARY 1/1 Bn Lan Fus

INTELLIGENCE SUMMARY

Army Form C. 2118.

Place	Date	Hour	Summary of Events and Information	Remarks and references to Appendices
ST DESPRED Gde HQs Wyk.	Jan 26 1917		Parade for Drug & Bayonet 9-15 AM 2-3 PM 2/Lt F.W. ANDERSER, 2/Lt WEYMAN rejoined bath from hospital with 14 ORs. PAS	
	27		Parade as yesterday. 2/Lt N.A. ABERNETHY, P. WALKER, J. McCREADY, T.A.W. KERR joined bath from ENGLAND with 156 OR. PAS	
	28		Parade — Holiday. PAS	
	29		Route march for Bn Hq & Drey at 8.30 AM to 12.30 PM. PAS	
	30		Church parade 6.30 AM. PAS	

G.S. Brown /Col
Comdg 1/1 Lan Fus.

30917

Confidential.

WAR DIARY
1/7 LAN. FUS
Oct. 1st–31st
1917.
—
Vol No. 30.

WAR DIARY of 1/7th LAN. FUS.
INTELLIGENCE SUMMARY

Army Form C. 2118.

Instructions regarding War Diaries and Intelligence Summaries are contained in F. S. Regs., Part II. and the Staff Manual respectively. Title pages will be prepared in manuscript.

(Erase heading not required.)

Place	Date 1917	Hour	Summary of Events and Information	Remarks and references to Appendices
ST. IDESBALD Camp	Oct 1		Bcoy & headquarters parade, 9.12, 2-3 P.M. P.A.S. Same on yesterday. P.A.S.	
Belgium 11. W.16/7	2		Parades as yesterday for Bcoy & headquarters. A & C coys return from 184th Tunnelling Coy RE. B coy remaining attached.	P.A.S
	3		Orders received to relieve 32nd Div on night 5/6.	P.A.S
	4		Bcoy returned from 184th Tunnelling Coy RE. Advance parties of 1 officer & 3 NCOs sent up to learn new line.	P.A.S
	5		Left camp 7.15 pm and proceeded by road to NIEUPORT. Coy and headquarters finished at M33b 60 35. Batt. relieves 2nd KOYLI. In support to S2 & 6 LF. Batln in Radan HQ M28c 88. Bcoy M28b 03. D M38d 0085 A coy M38c 9585.	P.A.S
NIEUPORT Belgium Is. M28	6		Coy attached to 6LF. Relief completed 11.30 P.M. No casualties, the night was a very quiet one except for a few heavy shells in NIEUPORT. 2/Lt CRAMMOND rejoined from hospital.	P.A.S
			Rain all morning. Very quiet. Carrying & working parties found at night. No casualties.	
	7		At 1 A.M. line altered back 1 down to rivulet line. Rain in morning, evening very quiet, a few heavy shells in NIEUPORT. Working parties found at night, wiring & digging. Casualties 2 Killed 2 wounded.	P.A.S
	8		REDAN shelled with field guns at dawn. Very quiet in afternoon. Working parties found at night, both wiring & digging. Casualties 4 killed 3 wounded. Relieves 5LF at night.	P.A.S
	9		Quiet morning. Occasional artillery fire. Loud firing in afternoon. Casualties nil	P.A.S
			Carrying parties 11.30 pm in right subsector of the line.	
	10		Relief completed 3.30 A.M. Quiet day except for heavy enemy bombardment of canal bridge from 5.20 to 6.30 pm. A & B coy in line from M23b 9. to 23 b 35 05, and in support D in support hq at M23a cent. C in reserve near tu by. Casualties 3 killed 3 wounded. Bn Hq at M 28 c 45/15. Line held by a series of posts, both in front line & in support. Very quiet night for relief, and quiet day. Casualties 3 Killed 2 wounded.	P.A.S

WAR DIARY
or
INTELLIGENCE SUMMARY.
(Erase heading not required.)

Army Form C. 2118.

Place	Date 1918	Hour	Summary of Events and Information	Remarks and references to Appendices
NIEUPORT Belgium 12. M2S	Feb 11		Usual shelling during day. In early morning patrol examined BAMBURGH POLDER M23d M24c and found it unoccupied at Western end. Quiet night. Casualties 7 wounded.	PPS
	12		Our front line trench mortared frequently. Area round by shells 4.30 – 5 p.m. Very wet day. Casualties 1 killed 1 wounded. 2/Lt WILLIAMS Jones trn from ENGLAND. Relieved by 5 LF at night	PPS
	13		Quiet day. Very wet and consequently ground to front very muddy. Casualties 1 wounded. Commencing 10 p.m.	PPS
	14		Relief completed 3.30 a.m. Bn. retired to its reserve positions in REDAN. All coys in their Assembly Positions. Working & wiring parties found at night. Weather much improved. Casualties 5 wounded	PPS
	15		Quiet day. Working & wiring parties found at night. Strength with bn 24 officers 587 men. Total strength 35 officers 777 OR. PPS Casualties 3 killed 16 wounded	C.K.
	16		Enemy artillery more active. 2/Lt WEYMAN died of wounds received on previous night. Working & wiring parties found at night. Casualties 2 Died of wounds 8 wounded	C.K.
	17		Officers of 127 Bde recce line on morning. The Battn relieved 5th L.F. in its former position in Right sub section C + D coys in the Front line. A coy in Support. B coy in Reserve. Relief completed 9.30 p.m. Quiet night. Casualties 3 wounded.	C.K.
	18		Enemy artillery activity increasing. NIEUPORT & the bridges heavily shelled. Our front & support lines trench mortared periodically. Digging & wiring at night. Casualties 7 wounded.	C.K.
	19		Quieter day. Two Bridges shelled between 5.30 & 6 p.m. Casualties 8 wounded	C.K.
	20		NIEUPORT heavily shelled in the early morning & area around B.N.B. Q in Co afternoon. Casualties 1 wounded	C.K.

WAR DIARY of 1/7th Lancashire Fusiliers

Army Form C. 2118.

INTELLIGENCE SUMMARY.

(Erase heading not required.)

Place	Date 1917	Hour	Summary of Events and Information	Remarks and references to Appendices
NIEUPORT BELGIUM. 12 M28	21st		Very quiet day. Relieved at night by 5th Manchesters. Relief hindered by difficult passage of the YSER bridges. Casualties nil. C.O.	
OOST-DUNKERKE 11.S.E. 10000	22nd		Relief completed 2.30 a.m. The Battalion proceeded by Companies via WULPEN to huts at CANADA CAMP, COXYDE. W18 8cent. 2/Lt ANDREWS joined Bn. from ENGLAND. C.O.	
	23rd		H20 in morning. Day spent in cleaning & smartening up. C.O. proceeded on leave to U.K. Major KNYVETT in command. 2/Lt PEARSON, 2/Lt JACOBY, 2/Lt ELLIOT & 2/Lt ASHWORTH join Bn. from ENGLAND. C.O.	
	24th		Fine cold day. H20 at night. D Coy provided large working party for R.E.'s at OOST-DUNKERKE C.O.	
	25th		Larger part of Bn. working under R.E.'s at OOST-DUNKERKE. Remainder continues training in camp. C.O.	
	26th		Cold weather continues. Bright day. Working party & training as on 25th. OOST-DUNKERKE shelled in the afternoon. Casualties 2 wounded. C.O.	
	27th		Usual working party & parades. C.K.	
	28th		Fine day. Working party at OOST-DUNKERKE shelled in the afternoon. Casualties 4 killed 9 wounded. C.O.	
KERKEPANNE	29th		Battalion proceeded to billets at LA PANNE in the morning, marching via W20 & R82 C.O.	

Army Form C. 2118.

WAR DIARY of 1/7th Lancashire Fusiliers
or
INTELLIGENCE SUMMARY.
(Erase heading not required.)

Instructions regarding War Diaries and Intelligence Summaries are contained in F. S. Regs., Part II. and the Staff Manual respectively. Title pages will be prepared in manuscript.

Place	Date	Hour	Summary of Events and Information	Remarks and references to Appendices
	30th		Training recommenced, mostly Musketry Practices, on show (W21)	
	31st		Bright day. Training continued. Bayonet Fighting, Bombing, & Tactical Schemes. Strength of Battalion (with Batt.) 24 Officers 539 o.r. Total Strength 36 Officers 739 o.r. E.C.	

J. Maynard Major
for Lt. Col.
Comdg. 1/7th Bn.

CONFIDENTIAL.

Vol 10

War Diary
of
1/7th Battn. Lancashire Fusiliers

Vol. No. 40

Nov. 1st to Nov. 30th

1917.

29.L
5 sheets

Original Copy

WAR DIARY of 1/7th Lancashire Fusiliers

Army Form C. 2118.

INTELLIGENCE SUMMARY.

(Erase heading not required.)

Place	Date	Hour	Summary of Events and Information	Remarks and references to Appendices
LA PANNE BELGIUM SHEET II 40000	Nov 1st	-	Battn continued training on shore - mostly musketry practice & tactical Schemes.	C.C.
	2nd	-	Battn Route March in morning LA PANNE - ADINKERKE - ST IDESBALDE - LA PANNE.	C.C.
	3rd		Gas Instruction & Recreational Training in afternoon	
			Festilian day training as on Nov. 1st. C.O. reported from leave. 1 O.R. casualties 1 wounded	C.C. C.C.
	4th		Parade Services in LA PANNE	C.C.
NIEUPORT BELGIUM 12 S.W. 20000	5th		Battn marched from LA PANNE at 6.30 p.m. to NIEUPORT (via WULPEN) & relieved 1/5th Manchesters as Support Battalion Coy 1/7th & 1/8th Manchesters in LOMBARDZYDE Sector. A, B & D Coys in the REDAN (M28 c 99 & M28 a 93) C Coy in NIEUPORT (M28 a 25.25) Bn H.Q. at RUBBER HOUSE (M28 c 88) Relief commenced 10 p.m. completed 1 am. Casualties nil	
	6th		Exceptionally quiet night. Casualties nil. Bn C.B.Q heavily shelled about 7 am Remainder of day quiet. 7th & 8th Manchesters relieved at night in front line by 5th & 6th Lan Fus respectively. Raking parties at night. Casualties nil	C.C. C.C.
	7th		Fairly quiet day. B" H.Q shelled 3 pm Working parties at night. Casualties 2 wounded	
	8th		Quiet day. Bn C.B.Q moved to NIEUPORT (M28 C 72.05) Troops carrying parties at night etc	C.C.
	9th		Enemy artillery & aircraft very active Working parties at night. Casualties 3 wounded.	C.C.

Original Copy

(2)

WAR DIARY of 1/7th Lancashire Fusiliers
INTELLIGENCE SUMMARY.

Army Form C. 2118.

(Erase heading not required.)

Instructions regarding War Diaries and Intelligence Summaries are contained in F. S. Regs., Part II. and the Staff Manual respectively. Title pages will be prepared in manuscript.

Place	Date	Hour	Summary of Events and Information	Remarks and references to Appendices
NIEUPORT BELGIUM SHEET 12 S.W. 1/20000	Nov. 10th	—	Reb day. Enemy artillery active at night. B" relieved 5th L.F. in front line. Right Subsector A + B Coys in front line (M.23.c.35.05 to M.22.b.88.12.) C. Coy in support in NASAL WALK (M.29.b.30.85 to M.29.a.0.2) D. Coy in Reserve in REDAN (M.23.c.99.88.) B" H.Q. at RUBBER HOUSE (M.23.c.89.) Relief completed 10.15pm. 8th L.F. on our left. 10th night. Casualties 1 O.R. w. 2 w. C.K.	
	11th	—	Very quiet day. NASAL WALK shelled in afternoon. Casualties 2 wounded C.K.	
	12th	—	Heavy British barrage on dusfront night at 3.30am. Gas shells into NIEUPORT at night. Casualties 4 wounded C.K.	
	13th	—	Quiet day. Little shelling. 2/Lt GREENHALGH rejoined B" from hospital. Casualties nil C.K.	
	14th	—	Another quiet day. Occasional shelling of NIEUPORT. B" relieved at night in front line by 5th L.F. + returned to previous position in Support (see Nov 5th + 7th) Relief commenced 5.30 pm. completed 9 pm. Casualties 1 killed 11 wounded C.K.	
	15th	—	FIVE BRIDGES shelled in morning. Day otherwise quiet. Strength of Batt" (with B") 23 Off. 49 O.R. Total strength 36 Off. 7 P. O.R. Carrying parties at night. Casualties nil. C.K.	
	16th	—	Exceptionally quiet day. 2/Lt GREENHALGH attached 125th M.G. Coy. Usual carrying parties at night. Casualties nil. C.K.	
	17th	—	Very quiet day. French advance parties arrived B" carrying S.A.A. etc. at night. Casualties 2 wounded C.K.	
	18th	—	Great arrival + artillery activity during day. Very quiet after 5 pm. Brigade relieved at night by French (321 Infy Regt. + 16th Chasseurs) B" was not relieved but marched out via PELICAN BRIDGE - WULPEN - OOST-DUNKERKE to huts at CANADA CAMP (W.1 & b.77) Night spent in cleaning up. Casualties 4 wounded C.K.	

Engraved Copy

(3)

WAR DIARY of 1/7th Lancashire Fusiliers

INTELLIGENCE SUMMARY

(Erase heading not required.)

Army Form C. 2118.

Instructions regarding War Diaries and Intelligence Summaries are contained in F.S. Regs., Part II. and the Staff Manual respectively. Title pages will be prepared in manuscript.

Place	Date	Hour	Summary of Events and Information	Remarks and references to Appendices
BELGIUM & FRANCE SHEET 18 1/40000	Nov. 19th		B[n] marched to ADINKERKE thence by barge to TETEGHEM ( ) B[n] H.Q at I.15.b.13.	G.K
DO SHEET 27 1/40000	20th		Clear day. B[n] marched at 9.45 am to billets at WARMHOUDT via BERGUES. B[n] H.Q. at C.10.d.9.1.	G.K
			CAPT BOYD rejoined from Hospital & 2/Lt WARDEN joined from ENGLAND	G.K
"	21st		Wet day. B[n] marched to billets in KIEKEN PUT + RIETVELD. B[n] H.Q. G.30.d.4.7.	G.K
"	22nd		B[n] continued march south to STAPLE and L'ANGE & ZUYDEZEELE arriving midday. Rest in afternoon. B[n] H.Q. VIBBE LAEQUIER 3 Sw. SE 2/Lt CHURCH	
FRANCE SHEET 36N 1/40000	23rd		Clear day. B[n] marched via WALLON-CAPPEL to billets in LES CISEAUX. B[n] H.Q. I.2.a.4.2.	G.K
	24th		joined B[n] from ENGLAND	G.K
			Day spent in cleaning up. 2/Lt HASSAL joined B[n] from ENGLAND	G.K
	25th		Clear cold day. B[n] morning Coys proceeded to baths at STEENBECQUE. Coy E. Parades	
			afternoon followed by games	G.K
	26th		Clear cold day. Day spent in reconnoitering up & preparing for move into line.	G.K
	27th		Clear day. Batt[n] marched to BETUNE via THIENNES, ST. VENANT + ROBECQ (distance 15 miles) H.K.
	28th		Batt[n] marched via BEUVRY to GUINCHY and relieved 11th CHESHIRE REGT. in Front Line. Right Central Sector. "A" Coy at A.22.a.0.6. to A.21.d.8.9. "C" Coy at A.27.b.6.5. "C" Coy at A.21.d.8.9. to A.21.d.6.3. and "D" Coy at A.21.d.0.6. to A.21.d.8.9. "B" Coy (in support) at A.21.a.8.7 to A.21.B.31. Batt[n] H.Q. at A.21.C.75.75. PORTUGUESE on Right, 8th L.F. on left. 6th L.F. in Support. Relief complete 12.15 pm. Casualties - nil	H.K.A

Army Form C. 2118.

WAR DIARY of 7/7th Lincolnshire Regt.
or
INTELLIGENCE SUMMARY.
(Erase heading not required.)

Instructions regarding War Diaries and Intelligence Summaries are contained in F. S. Regs., Part II. and the Staff Manual respectively. Title pages will be prepared in manuscript.

Place	Date	Hour	Summary of Events and Information	Remarks and references to Appendices
GUINCHY. Sheet 36c NW 1/10,000	29th		Clear day. Enemy artillery very quiet. Slight aerial activity. Casualties - nil.	NIL
	30th		Enemy artillery quiet during morning. Several gas shells fired by the enemy on our battery positions about 8.0 pm. Considerable artillery activity between 7.0 pm and 8-30 pm on the right of our sector. Slight aerial activity during the afternoon. Casualties - nil.	NIL

G.S. Bevin, Lt Col
Comdg 1/7 Linc Ins.

CONFIDENTIAL. W II

War Diary
1/7th Bn. Two.
1st – 31st December 1917

VOLUME ———— 41.

30.L
5 sheets

WAR DIARY of 1/7th Lancashire Fusiliers

INTELLIGENCE SUMMARY

Army Form C. 2118.

Place	Date	Hour	Summary of Events and Information	Remarks and references to Appendices
FRANCE 21A LA BASSÉE 36E N.W. 1/20,000	Dec 1st		First day TOWER RESERVE Blown in by large shell. Quiet day otherwise. Casualties nil	GK
	2nd		Wet in morning, clearing later. Casualties nil	GK
	3rd		Very quiet day. Advanced parties of 6th Lan Fus arrived. T.M. accidentally exploded in our lines killing 2 of its own Bn. Casualties nil	GK
FRANCE 36c N.W. 1/20,000	4th		Clear day. Battalion relieved by the 5th & 3rd Lancs Fus. and marched to billets at LE PREOL via CAMBRIN. Brigade Reserve. Casualties NIL. Relief commenced 10am Complete 1.30pm.	GK
	5th		Fine day cold. Day spent in smartening up drill and general cleaning up	H&A
	6th		Battalion carried out Training Programme cholests Drill, Bombing. Enemy bombs dropped on BETHUNE district	H&A
	7th		Battalion continued Training (as on 6th) Rugby eleven (6 v 7th) East Lancashire Regt.	H&A
	8th		"Clear and fine". 2nd and Lieut. Payne joined from England. Afternoon spent in preparing for move.	H&A
FRANCE 36A S.E. 1/20,000	9th		Battalion marched to HINGETTE via LES GAUDRONS afterwards which by 4th East Lancashire Regt. (Corps Reserve) Relief commenced at 1115 am Complete by 12 noon. Billets at W.17.d.0.9.	GK
	10th		Fine day. Day spent in improving billets	GK
	11th		Battalion carried out Training Programme chiefly Musketry and Squad drill. 2/Lt Thorpe reported from Base to 9/Lt 2nd 9th End of Coys. and the T.O. reconnoitered SWITCH LINE. All Billets were inspected by the M.O.	H&A

WAR DIARY 1/7 Lancashire Fusiliers
INTELLIGENCE SUMMARY

Army Form C. 2118.

Place	Date	Hour	Summary of Events and Information	Remarks and references to Appendices
FRANCE 36ª SE 20000	Dec 12th		Battalion continued training Programme with Musketry and Bayonet Training	6/6
	13th		Fine and cold. Training Programme carried out including firing on Range. Afternoon devoted to Recreational Training. Major Konyott detailed to g'Hards Bn Regt.	6/6
	14th		Cold and dull. Bn continued Training Programme including firing on Range and Lewis Gun Instruction.	6/6
	15th		Fine cold. Heavy enemy heard to NE direction. Enemy shelled BETHUNE – Three Sheright.	6/6
			Offrs: 41 OR 661	
	16th		Fine cold – Training Programme carried out. Inter Platoon Competition organised – Preliminary Heats	6/6
	17th		Fine and clear. A B & C Coys on working Parties. D Coy carried out Training Programme including Gas Drill. Lt Peirhous wounded from Sniping Post 4" Any.	6/6
	18th		Cold weather continuing. A B & C coys provided working parties for front areas. Remainder of Bn carried out Training Programme. 2/Lt BROWN joined Bn from ENGLAND	6/6
	19th		Battln Xmas Day Festivities fêted. Company officials in morning. Garrison afternoon	6/6
	20th		Cold weather continuing. A B & D coys provided working parties for RE's in front area. Remainder of Battln carrying on training. Football in afternoon	6/6
	21st		Coys proceeded to Baths & prepared for move on following day	6/6

WAR DIARY of 1/5th Lancashire Fusiliers

INTELLIGENCE SUMMARY

Army Form C. 2118.

(Erase heading not required.)

Place	Date	Hour	Summary of Events and Information	Remarks and references to Appendices
FRANCE 36c NW 10000	22nd		Cold weather continuing. Bn marched via LES CHOQUAUX and GORRE to GIVENCHY and relieved 7th Manchesters in Right Subsector of Left Section. B.A. and C Coys in	
			front line (Aq9.7. A3q.6.) D Coy in support (Aq9.3.) Bn H.Q at A8dq.5. 10 Manchesters in right 8th Lan Fus on left. 5th Lan Fus in support. Relief commenced	CR
		11.30 am	completed 1.30 pm. Quiet day. Casualties nil	CR
	23rd		Very quiet day. Casualties: 1 killed, 1 wounded	
	24th		Cold bright day. Considerable artillery activity. At night gas was projected into enemy lines from the Right Section. Followed by two sharp bombardments. Considerable damage to enemy trenches. Enemy retaliation weak. Cas. nil	CR
	25th		Clear day & extremely bright night. Much enemy movement observed & good work carried out by our snipers. Cas. nil	CR
	26th		Bright day. Artillery quiet. Much aerial activity. Good opportunities for sniping. Cas: one of our prisoners	CR
	27th		Cold day. Very quiet. Cas nil	CR
	28th		Bn relieved by 5th Lan Fus & proceeded to support. A Coy garrisoned GIVENCHY KEEP, HAIRIES, HULDERS and HERTS REDOUBTS and MOAT FARM. C Coy in support to 6th Lan Fus at B3. HQ, B, & 7 D Coys at WINDY CORNER (Arc.8.3) Cas: 1 killed (2/Lt Williams) by 2 & 6 Lew)	CR
	29th		During morning HERTS REDOUBT shelled in afternoon 3 dunchies carried.	CR

WAR DIARY of 1/7th Lancashire Fusiliers. **Army Form C. 2118.**
or
INTELLIGENCE SUMMARY.
(Erase heading not required.)

Instructions regarding War Diaries and Intelligence Summaries are contained in F. S. Regs., Part II. and the Staff Manual respectively. Title pages will be prepared in manuscript.

Place	Date	Hour	Summary of Events and Information	Remarks and references to Appendices
FRANCE 36℅ N.W 20000	Dec. 30th		Quiet day GIVENCHY KEEP shelled in afternoon. Cas nil	66
	31st		Cold weather continuing. Quiet day. GIVENCHY KEEP again lightly shelled. Cas 2 wounds.	66
			Total strength of Bn at O.R. 660. O.R. Killed Bn 29. O.R. 49 O.R.	
			Jan 1st 1918	
			G. S. Brain to Lt. Col	
			Cdg 1/7 Lancashire Fusiliers	

Confidential.

WAR - DIARY

of

1/7 Batt'n Lancashire Fusiliers

1st - 31st January 1918

Vol No 42.

WAR DIARY of 1/7th Lancashire Fusiliers

or INTELLIGENCE SUMMARY.

Army Form C. 2118.

(Erase heading not required.)

Instructions regarding War Diaries and Intelligence Summaries are contained in F. S. Regs., Part II. and the Staff Manual respectively. Title pages will be prepared in manuscript.

Place	Date 1918 Jan.	Hour	Summary of Events and Information	Remarks and references to Appendices
FRANCE 36c N.W. 1 20000	1st		Quiet day. Enemy fired large number of gas shells into sector on our right at night. Cas nil	C.K.
	2nd		Raw settling in. Quiet day. Major Knyvett reported 13th Bn commencing 9th Manchester. Cas nil	C.K.
			Cold at night. A few gas shells into sector on our right about midnight. Cas nil. O.K.	
	3rd		Cold bright day. B" relieved 5th Lan Fus in positions previously occupied on Right Subsection B, A + C Coys in Front line (A9d72 - A3c92) D Coy in Support (A9d73) B" H.Q. A6d95. 7th Manchesters on right, 8th Lan Fus on left. 6th Lan Fus in Support. Relief commenced 9.30 am completed 11.30 am. Heavy bombardment of Herts Ave (about A6d84) believed 2 pm to 3 pm. Major Knyvett assumed command of 5th Lan Fus the whole of the Headquarters staff of that unit having been gassed last night. Casualties 1 wounded.	(AG73) C.K.
	4th		Very quiet day. Considerable aircraft activity. Major Edge reported B" from 42nd Div at Hing Edo 1 w. Cas nil	C.K.
	5th		Another quiet day. Our patrols active at night. Cas nil	C.K.
	6th		Slight artillery activity. Cas nil	C.K.
	7th		Enemy T.M. bombardment on our right. Tabin gas alarm at 3 pm. Cas 3 wounded. C.K.	
	8th		A few 4.2.s round B" H.Q. in early morning. Quiet day otherwise. Cas 2 killed 2 wounded	C.K.
	9th		B" relieved by 5th Lan Fus & marched to billets at GORRE CHATEAU. Relief commenced 9.30 am completed 11.45 am. Snow in afternoon. Cas nil	C.K.

WAR DIARY of 1/7 Lancashire Fusiliers

Army Form C. 2118.

INTELLIGENCE SUMMARY.
(Erase heading not required.)

Place	Date	Hour	Summary of Events and Information	Remarks and references to Appendices
FRANCE 36B NE 1/20000	Jan 10th		Day spent in cleaning up, bathing & refitting. Bn afternoon 3 direct hits on Bde H.Q. at LOISNE with many casualties. 600 in Bn. 1 killed	6R
	11th		Wet day with few intervals. Training & bathing in morning. Remainder training in afternoon. Concert at night	6R
	12th		Cold day. Buckley & Stall in morning, games in afternoon. A few shells on GORRE in afternoon. 600 2 wounded	6R
	13th		Day clean day. Parade Service in morning. Sports at night.	6R
	14th		Snow in morning. Throwing Colin Buckley & Steadying dulls in morning from 12 noon	6R
	15th		Wet day. Indoor lectures. Strength of Bn. Total 40 off 661 OR. Killed Bn 28 off 603 OR	6R
	16th		Stormy day. Bn. provided working parties for RE. at WINDY CORNER	6R
	17th		Wet day. Bn. relieved 2nd Battalion by 5th E Lancs & marched into billets at BEUVRY	6R
	18th		Bn. reoccs Bn HQ at F14c.50.60. A Coy F14a.6̄.25 B, C, + D Coys F14c.80.20. Road buffs	6R
	19th		Day spent in cleaning up. 3 Coys provide working parties for REs at CAMBRIN. A Coy on Range	6R
	20th		Fine day. 3 Coys provide working parties as on 18th. Remainder bathing in morning. Range in afternoon	6R
	21st		Parade Services in morning. Games in afternoon. Concert at night	6R
	22nd		4 Coys find working parties for REs at CAMBRIN. Clear day. Working parties as on 21st	6R

Instructions regarding War Diaries and Intelligence Summaries are contained in F.S. Regs., Part II. and the Staff Manual respectively. Title pages will be prepared in manuscript.

WAR DIARY of 1/7 Lancashire Fusiliers
INTELLIGENCE SUMMARY.
(Erase heading not required.)

Army Form C. 2118.

Place	Date	Hour	Summary of Events and Information	Remarks and references to Appendices
	23rd		Dull day. Working parties on 20, 21st. Details employed at meals by U.S. Major Boyce	GK
	24th		Bright day. Working parties as at 21st. Concert at night	GK
	25th		Fine day. Working parties as at 21st. Bethune bombed at night by E.A.	GK
	26th		Fine clear day. Working parties as usual. Concert at night	GK
	27th		Fine day. Battery Parade Service in morning. Company cooking competition won by A Coy. Kit-laying competition by H.Q. Coy. Games in afternoon. Concert at night	GK
	28th		Bright clear day. Companies training in Busnettes. Hockey etc. preparing for snow on following day. Enemy aircraft over Bethune about 11.30 and	GK
FRANCE 36 a N.W. 30002	29th		Bright day. B" marched into the line via Cambrin & relieved 6th Manchesters in Canal Sector. Right subsector. A Coy at Arthur B Coy at A21c 6d C Coy at A21c 6d D Coy at A15 b 6 b - H.Q. A21c 97. Relief commenced 10.45 and completed 2 p.m. Coy quiet day. Casualties nil.	GK
	30th		Misty day. Coy quiet. N.G. fairly active at night. E.A. brought down in flames at A16 a 20.30 Coy MG [?]	GK
	31st		Cold misty day. Coy quiet. A few T.M.s round the Mich in morning. About midnight enemy attempted a raid on the Portuguese sector but was repulsed. Gas nil. Strength of B" Total 30 off. 705 O.R. With B" 28 off. 530 O.R.	GK

In the Field
1.2.18

J.S. Brain. Lieut Colonel
Commanding 1/7 Lancashire Fusiliers

CONFIDENTIAL.

WAR DIARY of
1/7 Batt. LANCASHIRE
FUSILIERS

FEB. 1918

Vol 33.

WAR DIARY of 1/7 Lancashire Fusiliers

INTELLIGENCE SUMMARY

Army Form C. 2118.

Feb 1918.

Place	Date	Hour	Summary of Events and Information	Remarks and references to Appendices
FRANCE N.E. 36.B 1:20000	Feb 1st		Quiet day. Excellent patrol work at night under 2/Lts WALKER & ELLIOT. Cas. nil	CR
	2nd		Bright day. Number of enemy shells about Bn. HQ & the LANE. Further good patrolling at night by 2/Lts WALKER & ELLIOT. Cas. nil	CR
	3rd		Clear day. Bn relieved by 5th Lan. Fus. & marched into billets at LE PREOL vco	CR
			ANNEQUIN Bn Reserve. Relief commenced 10.30 am, completed 11.45 am. Bn HQ at 7.15b12. Cas. nil. Remainder of day spent in cleaning up.	CR
	4th		Bn provided working parties for the line. Cas nil	CR
	5th		Bright day. Working parties again provided.	CR
	6th		Clear day. Working parties for the line. Bathing in afternoon	CR
	7th		Dull drizzling day. Working parties as usual. Lieut F.B. WEBB proceeded to ENGLAND for six months.	CR
FRANCE - LA BASSEE 1:10000	8th		Feb morning, clearing later. Bn marched to CAMBRIN & relieved 5th Lan. Fus. in Right Bn Sector. Right Sub sector in positions previously occupied (Jan 29th) Relief commenced 3 p.m. completed 4.30 pm. Cas nil	CR
	9th		Quiet day. Good patrol work at night. Cas nil	CR
	10th		Artillery more active. 2/Lt CHURCH wounded & died of wounds later. 1 O.R. missing	CR

WAR DIARY of 1/7th Lancashire Fusiliers

INTELLIGENCE SUMMARY
Army Form C. 2118.

(Erase heading not required.)

Place	Date	Hour	Summary of Events and Information	Remarks and references to Appendices
LA BASSEE 1:10000	11th		Bright day. 2/Lt WALKER M.C. searched No Man's Land in daylight Cas nil. Good patrol work at night by 2/Lt ELLIOTT. Cas nil.	GK
	12th		Quiet day. At midnight 2/Lt ELLIOTT assisted by R.E.s successfully blew up hostile mineshaft in enemy line at A.22.C.8.9. Cas nil.	GK
	13th		Quiet day. Occasional shelling of THE LANE. Cas nil	GK
	14th		About 11.30 am enemy fired large number of gas shells in BN HQ. In the afternoon Bn was relieved by 2/6d & 7th L.F. 7th L.F. relieved by 2/5 L.F. Bn marched via BEUVRY to billets in	GK
FRANCE 36B N.E. 1:20000	15th		FOUQUIERES E 21 a & b. Relief commenced 2 pm completed 4 pm. Cas nil. Brigade paraded at VERQUIN where 6th L.F. marched past prior to being disbanded. Remainder of day spent in cleaning up. 2/Lts CHADWICK, PROCTOR, MORGAN T. FREDERICKS, + 120 O.R. joined Bn from 6th L.F. Total strength of Bn 44 off 855 or	GK
	16th		Cold day. Reorganizing & cleaning up. C.S.M. BOLLAND awarded Croix de Guerre	GK
	17th		Coy: find working parties for wiring E. of BETHUNE. Parade service in morning Col DETAILS Lt. Col. BREWIS proceed on leave to U.K. MAJOR KNYVETT assumes command of Bn	GK
	18th		Clear cold day. Working parties found by A, B, & C Coys. Remainder training. Football in afternoon. Bn concert at night	GK

WAR DIARY of 1/7th Lancashire Fusiliers Battalion

INTELLIGENCE SUMMARY

Army Form C. 2118.

(Erase heading not required.)

Place	Date	Hour	Summary of Events and Information	Remarks and references to Appendices
FRANCE 36 N.E. 1:20000	19th		Training in Musketry, Close Order Drill, Bombing etc. A & B Coys on Range. Representation from Bn proceeded to CHOCQUES STN. to bid Farewell to 6th L.F. 2/Lt BAILEY joined Bn from 6th L.F.	CK CK
	20th		Training continued. Demonstration on moving by specially trained platoon. Draft of 53 O.R. from "E" I.B.D.	CK
	21st		Training continued. Lieut E.W. SPINK proceeded to U.K. for 6 months tour of duty.	CK
	22nd		Training continued. Demonstration platoon again gave demonstration on moving.	CK
			Recreational training in afternoon.	
	23rd		Clear day. Bn Route march in morning. FOUQUEREUIL – CHOCQUES – LABEUVRIÈRE – FOUQUIÈRES.	CK
			Football in afternoon. Draft of 18 O.R. from "K" I.B.D. 2/Lt ELLIOTT awarded M.C.	CK
	24th		Parade Services in morning. Demonstration by platoon of H.A.C. in afternoon. 2/Lt BAILEY att. D.H.Q.	CK
	25th		Wet morning. Clearing bales. Lectures on War Savings in morning H.Q. Officers & Coy Commanders reconnoitre SAILLY-LABOURSE LOCALITY.	CK
	26th		Training continued. 2 days War Saving campaign opened. Football in afternoon. Concert at night.	CK
	27th		Training continued. War Saving Campaign closed.	CK
			Clear cold day. Lieut Kershaw proceded on leave to U.K.	HA

WAR DIARY
or
INTELLIGENCE SUMMARY.

(Erase heading not required.)

Army Form C. 2118.

Place	Date	Hour	Summary of Events and Information	Remarks and references to Appendices
FRANCE 36 NE 1:20000	7th 28		Clear day. Training continued - A Coy on Range. Recreational Training in afternoon.	14A

42nd Division.
125th Infantry Brigade.

1/7th BATTALION

LANCASHIRE FUSILIERS

MARCH 1 9 1 8

33.L
6 sheets

Vol 14

CONFIDENTIAL 125/4/2

WAR DIARY

OF

1/7 BATT LANCS FUS.

VOL. 44

1st – 31st MARCH 1918.

WAR DIARY 1st 1/7th B" LANCASHIRE FUSILIERS Army Form C. 2118.

INTELLIGENCE SUMMARY.

(Erase heading not required.)

Place	Date	Hour	Summary of Events and Information	Remarks and references to Appendices
FRANCE 36B NE 1:20000	MAR 1st		Training Programme continued. Musketry, Gas Drill – special attention to rapid adjustment of box respirators. 2nd Lieut E. Chadwick proceeded to Base unfit. Captain C.E. Fitzgerald MC to 1st Balloon Wing H.9 R.F.C. Recreational Training in afternoon. Heavy firing heard NE this morning.	HEA
	2nd		The Battalion moved to Billets at TOUQUERTOIL – "B" Hqrs at E.14.c.4.2.	
	3rd		Morning spent in cleaning up, organth. and preparing for the move. All Coys paraded for demonstration by Platoon of I.A.C. Attack on Strong Point practised in morning. Afternoon Platoon Bayonet fighting also Recreational Training.	HEA
	4th		Training Programme continued including Musketry on the Range. Recreational Training in afternoon. Heavy firing heard again at NE during night and early morning.	HEA
	5th		Training Programme as for the 4th instant. Recreational Training in afternoon. Lieut Col G.S. Brews-mount command of Battalion vice Major J.S. Knipe on relicy from [illeg.] leave to U.K.	HEA
	6th		Training Programme continued. A & B Coys on Range in morning. Range E.19.a Special attention given to range discipline. FESTUBERT-TUNING FORK-FRONT LINE reconnoitred – 2nd Lt W. Steele returned from leave to U.K. [illeg.]	HEA
	7th		Training Programme carried out. Including Wiring Musketry, Bayonet Fighting – Recreational Training	[illeg.]

WAR DIARY / INTELLIGENCE SUMMARY

1/7 B" Lancashire Fusiliers Army Form C. 2118.

Place	Date	Hour	Summary of Events and Information	Remarks and references to Appendices
FRANCE 36 N.E 1:20,000	MAR 7th		in afternoon. Heavy firing heard in N.E. direction in early morning.	HRA
	8th		Training continued on No 13 Area. Platoon Tactical Schemes. Fire Discipline. Gas and Bill Drill. Recreational training in afternoon.	HRA
	9th		Sunday. Usual Parade Services. Fine and warm day. Summer Time comes into operation at 11 p.m. Clocks put forward one hour.	HRA
	10th		Days Training carried out - Attacking Demonstration in attacking a Strong Point - afterwards practised.	HRA
	11th		In Coys. Recreational Training in afternoon.	HRA
	12th		The Battalion found a Working Party of 5 Officers and 350 OR burying a Cable W. of ANNEQUIN. Training Programme carried out - Including a Tactical Scheme at E.19.a.2.b. Recreational Training in afternoon.	PJS
	13th		Training Programme as above - Including "Company in the Attack" "Gas Drill. Bill drill Recreational Training in afternoon.	PJS
	14th		3 Companies Bayonet Fighting Arm Drill Musketry etc. Officers and NCO's on construction of Aeroplanes.	PJS
	15		A Coy on Range No 14. B.C & D Coys carried out Training Programme. Strength of battalion Officers 27. OR 878.	PJS

Army Form C. 2118.

WAR DIARY of 1/5 Lon ?
INTELLIGENCE SUMMARY.
(Erase heading not required.)

Instructions regarding War Diaries and Intelligence Summaries are contained in F.S. Regs., Part II. and the Staff Manual respectively. Title pages will be prepared in manuscript.

Place	Date	Hour	Summary of Events and Information	Remarks and references to Appendices
FRANCE FONQUEREL	Mar 16		Route in vicinity of billets in morning. Bde. boxing competition	App
	.17.		Bde. parade for decoration of Medal Ribbons by Maj. Gen. Solly-Flood CMG DSO Comdg. 42 Div.	App
	.18.		Demonstration by B Coy to rest of Battalion of the attack in all stages from artillery formation	App
			to halting of a firing line. Day removed from billets to an adjacent camp.	
	.19.		Training under Coy arrangements	App
	.20.		Runs in morning. Bayonet demonstration at Leivre in afternoon	App
	.21.		Training under Coy arrangements.	App
	.22.		Bde. platoon, trench clearing, musketry competition. Orders received 10.30pm to prepare for a	App
			move.	
	.23.		Batt. marched out 8.0 AM to HESDIGNEUL where it entrained and proceeded via BRUAY,	
			ST.POL, DOULLENS, BEAUMETZ to ADINFER, bivouacking the night in the wood (57D F1.2)	App
	.24.		Left ADINFER WOOD 3pm & marched to LoEAST WOOD (57 A 25.26) remaining to dark after	App
			which batt. marched via COMIECOURT & AYL to BEHAGNIES H12	
	.25.		Arrived BEHAGNIES district 2 AM to relieve 40 Div. whose position could not be located.	
			Batt. took up strong defensive position between SAPIGNIES (H8) & E. HUCOURT H 9 1/2 N. K.	
			1/7 Lde. on right, 5LF on left. Stragglers from 40 & 41 Divs were also utilised in defensive	App
			position.	

INTELLIGENCE SUMMARY.

WAR DIARY
or
INTELLIGENCE SUMMARY.
(Erase heading not required.)

Army Form C. 2118.

Place	Date	Hour	Summary of Events and Information	Remarks and references to Appendices
	Mar 25		At 8 A.M. enemy attacked whole div. front and was held up until about 9 A.M. when withdrawal was necessary owing to both flanks being turned and heavy enfilade fire being brought upon position. Retirement was carried out in perfect order, to prepared positions in rear. Again owing to flanks giving way enemy succeeded in surrounding our position, which were dominated on everyside, + heavy loss was inflicted on the enemy. Casualties 5 Killed 74 wounded 64 missing.	O.S.
	26		Batt. was ordered to withdraw to LOGEAST WOOD at 12 midnight (25-26) this time enemy were at close quarters all round our position + withdrawal was not carried out until 2.0 A.M. aft. beating off an attack. Withdrawal was again carried out in perfect order. Later bath. formed up as artillery formation + marched to LOGEAST WOOD where it rested from 3 A.M. to 6 A.M. Owing to approach of enemy a further withdrawal was ordered at 6.00 A.M. Batt. marched via ABLAINZEVILLE, F 23 e.A. BUCQUOY to a prearranged outpost position behind BUCQUOY E 21 c + d meeting 137 + 136 Bdes. Carried out rearguard action + finally took up defensive position on line BUCQUOY - ABLAINZEVILLE. 63rd Div on right to the of GUARDS on left. Weather Khes [unclear]	O.S.

WAR DIARY or INTELLIGENCE SUMMARY.

Army Form C. 2118.

Place	Date	Hour	Summary of Events and Information	Remarks and references to Appendices
	May 27		Batt. in same position i.e. in outpost position occupied by 1/5 L.F.a. The line was thinly maintained in spite of 2 enemy attacks on 1/5 L.F.a. 1 Killed. 1 died of wounds.	P.P.S
	28.		Same position maintained.	P.P.S
	29.		Enemy attacks 1/5/6 L.F.a. Batt sent to reinforce & occupied position in sunken road in Fight. Enemy attack failed. At 9 p.m. batt relieved 5 & 7 L/Mks in line (Brigade left sub-sect) 1 wounded.	P.P.S
	30.		Position shelled intermittently. Enemy did not attack. Batt relieved by 26 R.Fus. (4th Div) P.P.S. Position of batt in reserve. 1 wounded.	P.P.S
	31.		Marched to trenches near GOMMECOURT (5° Exba). Position of batt in reserve. 1 wounded. Strength of batt 23 Officers 731 O.R.	P.P.S

D. Morton LT. COL.
BDG. 1/7 LANCASHIRE FUSILIERS.

125th Inf.Bde.
42nd Div.

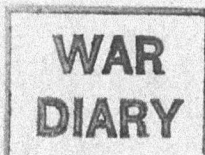

1/7th BATTN. THE LANCASHIRE FUSILIERS.

A P R I L

1 9 1 8

CONFIDENTIAL

Vol 15
125/42

34.L
5 shelves

WAR DIARY

VOL. 4-5

1/7th BATT. LANCS. FUS.

1 - 30 APRIL. 1918

Army Form C. 2118.

WAR DIARY
of 1/7th BATT. LANCASHIRE FUSILIERS
INTELLIGENCE SUMMARY.

(Erase heading not required.)

Instructions regarding War Diaries and Intelligence Summaries are contained in F. S. Regs., Part II. and the Staff Manual respectively. Title pages will be prepared in manuscript.

Place	Date	Hour	Summary of Events and Information	Remarks and references to Appendices
FRANCE.	APL			
Battn. H.Q.	1st		Battn in trenches near GOMMECOURT 57.8. E.29.a.x.b. position of Batln in Divisnl. Reserve	R.B.
That 57D E29a8b	2nd		On the night 2/3rd the Battn relieved the 26th R.Two (113th Divn) in front line at BUCQUOY. Left out sector, with the 126 Bde on the left and the 8th Lan Fus on the right. The Battn was organised in depth in a series of posts giving each other mutual support.	R.B.
	3rd		Position unchanged. Day fairly quiet.	R.B.
	4th		Position unchanged. Hostile artillery activity increased towards the evening.	R.B.
	5th		At 4.30 a.m. enemy put down heavy barrage on position occupied by 8th Lan Fus, also on support trenches. Heavy enemy fire was kept up during the greater part of the morning. The 8th Lan Fus on our right were forced to give some ground. The line occupied by the Battalion remained intact. Heavy casualties were inflicted on the enemy by our right and right centre companies. About 4 p.m. touch was gained with 5th Lan Fus and 8th Lan Fus on our right, and the situation became more settled and a definite line was re-established	R.B.

Army Form C. 2118.

WAR DIARY
of 1/7 LANCASHIRE FUSILIERS
INTELLIGENCE SUMMARY

(Erase heading not required.)

Place	Date	Hour	Summary of Events and Information	Remarks and references to Appendices
FRANCE	APL			
Batt. H.Q.	6th.		Situation unchanged. Our artillery shelled the positions newly won by the enemy in BUCQUOY Village. On night 6/7th the Battn was relieved by the 7th MANCHESTER REGT. and proceeded to trenches in support at 57D.F.26.b.	KB
Sheet 57D.				
F.26.d.9.6.	7th.		Our artillery broke up enemy attack which was seen developing in front of BUCQUOY Village. Situation on the whole quiet. The Battalion was relieved by detachments of 5th and 7th WEST YORKS REGT. (37 Division) The 37th Division took over the Divisional Front. The Battn marched via CONTLECOURT - FONQUEVILLERS - SOUASTRE and embused at the last named place.	KB
	8th.		Battn debussed at MARIEUX AERODROME at 6 a.m. and moved to VAUCHELLES at 6 p.m. and occupied CORPS INFANTRY SCHOOL. Draft of 9 Officers and 132 ot̲h̲s̲. from Glos. & War. Regt. joined Battalion.	KB
Batt. H.Q.	9th.		Day spent in Bathing, cleaning up and checking of deficiencies.	KB
Corps School	10th.		Same as previous day. Draft of 100 oths. (5th Kings L'pool Regt.) joined Batt.	KB
VAUCHELLES	11th.		Same as previous day.	KB

WAR DIARY of 1/7 BATT. LANCASHIRE FUSILIERS
INTELLIGENCE SUMMARY
(Erase heading not required.)

Army Form C. 2118.

Place	Date	Hour	Summary of Events and Information	Remarks and references to Appendices
FRANCE	12th		Divisional Commanders inspection	
	13th		At 9.30 a.m. moved into billets at ST. LEGER. Training grounds allotted	
			Coys at disposal of Coy. Commanders	
	14th	11.0 a.m.	Church Parade. Musketry training by companies	
	15th		Squad & Company Drill 2 hours. Musketry training 2 hours. Part of the line to be taken over from the 1st ESSEX REGT. reconnoitred	
	16th	At 5.30 p.m.	Battn. proceeded to support trenches at GOMMECOURT PARK marching via BAYENCOURT	
Batt. H.Q.	17th		Relieved 1st ESSEX REGT. in support at GOMMECOURT PARK at 2 a.m.	
K 3 d. 9. 9.	18th		Poor visibility. Early stand to ordered. Men rested during day	
	19th		Slight fall of snow in morning. All coys making battle positions during night.	
	20th		Poor visibility. Enemy very quiet. Coys working on battle positions during night.	
	21st		Coys clearing trenches and wiring during night. Enemy artillery fairly active.	

Army Form C. 2118.

WAR DIARY
or
INTELLIGENCE SUMMARY.
of 1/7 BATT. LANCASHIRE FUSILIERS
(Erase heading not required.)

Place	Date	Hour	Summary of Events and Information	Remarks and references to Appendices
FRANCE	APL. 22nd		Improvement of battle positions continued at night	&c
	23rd		Situation very quiet. Work proceeded with at night. Our artillery active	&c
	24th		Artillery on both sides very quiet. Trenches improved	&c
	25th		Poor visibility. Work on trench improvement continued during night. MAJOR CADE R.H. rejoined the Batt.	&c
	26th		Poor visibility. C.O. awarded Bar to D.S.O. LT. KERSHAW C. and 2T. BREWIS R.K. awarded M.C.s. Eight N.M.s awarded three D.C.M.s awarded.	&c
	27th		Visibility improved. Situation quiet. Usual work of wiring etc at night	&c
	28th		The Batt. was relieved by 1/7 MANCHESTER REGT. and proceeded to Reserve Bde Area in 57D J6&4d (near CHATEAU-DE-LA-HAIE)	&c
Batt. HQ.	29th		Arrived at CHATEAU-DE-LA-HAIE about 2 a.m. Batta rested during day.	&c
J6.d.	30th		Batt. on working parties. CAPT.B.SHERMERDINE, 2T. MURGATROYD H.I. and 2T. GOULD H.M. & 2/LT. ASHWORTH J.E. awarded M.C.s. 1/c FRIMSTONE and PTE PETRIE awarded D.C.M.s	&c

Murgatroyd Major
2 Lieut Colonel
Commdg 1/7 Lancashire Fusiliers

WAR DIARY

VOL. 46

1/7th BATTN LAN. FUS.

1–31st MAY 1918

WAR DIARY of 1/1st Bn. Lancashire Fusiliers

or INTELLIGENCE SUMMARY.

(Erase heading not required.)

Army Form C. 2118.

Place	Date	Hour	Summary of Events and Information	Remarks and references to Appendices
FRANCE Sheet 51PNE 1:20,000 Bn. H.Q. J6d.3.9etm.	May 1st		Battalion on working parties. Line reconnoitred. Dugouts improved.	W.F.B.
	2nd		Lt. Murgatroyd and 2/Lieut. Green left Battalion to join 2nd Lancashire Fusiliers. 10th Manchesters took over. Battalion relieved 6th Manchesters in line.	W.F.B.
Bn. H.Q. K6 & 85.65	3rd		Enemy very quiet during day. He put down heavy barrage between Biez Wood and Rossignol Wood at 7.30 p.m. Battalion improving positions during night. 1 killed, 5 wounded. Improvements to line continued.	W.F.B.
	4th			W.F.B.
Bn. H.Q. K6a 3.5 & 45.94	5th		As yesterday. Changed Battalion H.Q. at 7.0.p.m. 1 Killed, 2 wounded.	W.F.B.
	6th		Major Marshall wounded. Battalion relieved by 2/6th Kings Liverpools. 1 Killed.	W.F.B.
Bn HQ T2a. 25.65	7th		Arrived Gouin Wood about 6 A.M. Rested during day.	W.F.B.
	8th		Cleaning up, making up deficiencies, and paying out.	W.F.B.
	9th		Practiced "Battle positions in Line (L.H. Halle (Purple)	W.F.B.
	10th		Battalion training according to programme. Capt. B. Shelmerdine. M.C. rejoined from 125 Brigade H.Q.	W.F.B.

WAR DIARY of 1/7th Bn. LANCASHIRE FUSILIERS

INTELLIGENCE SUMMARY

Army Form C. 2118.

(Erase heading not required.)

Place	Date	Hour	Summary of Events and Information	Remarks and references to Appendices
FRANCE 57d NE Sheet 57d.Ba 35.66. Bn H.Q.	May 11th		Traversed Battle Position on LA HAIE TURPLE LINE.	W.G.B.
	12"		Church Parade. Training in musketry.	W.G.B.
	13"		Practice attack by two companies at which Army Commander was present. One Company supplied working party for LA HAIE SWITCH. Remainder of Battalion training in musketry etc.	W.G.B.
	14"		Training, musketry, physical drill, bayonet fighting and open warfare. One Company supplied working party for BAYENCOURT SWITCH. Lecture on British Tanks. LA HAIE SWITCH.	W.G.B.
	15"		Training in Trench and Open warfare. Strength 33 Officers, 964 other ranks.	W.G.B.
	16"		Signalling Scheme. One Company working on BAYENCOURT SWITCH. Remainder of Battalion Training as above.	W.G.B.
	17"		Training and working parties as above. Lecture to all officers by Brigadier General.	W.G.B.
	19"		Church Parade. Companies marched to PAS and back in full marching order. Bathing at PAS.	W.G.B.

WAR DIARY of 1/7th Bn LANCASHIRE FUSILIERS

INTELLIGENCE SUMMARY

(Erase heading not required.)

Place	Date	Hour	Summary of Events and Information	Remarks and references to Appendices
FRANCE Sheet 57DNE Bn H.Q. T29.95.45	MAY 20th		Working parties for BAYENCOURT SWITCH. Training in musketry, bayonet fighting, bombing. Physical drill etc.	W.S.B.
	21st		Training. Companies carried out collective attacking. Battalion bayonet contest.	W.S.B. W.S.B.
	22nd		Working parties and training as above.	W.S.B.
	23rd		Working parties and training as above.	W.S.B.
	24th		Working parties and training as above.	W.S.B.
	25th		Working parties and training as above. 2/LIEUT C. LYMIE rejoined Battalion from Divisional Signal School.	W.S.B.
	26th		Practice Battle Positions in LA HAIG PURPLE LINE at 4 a.m. Church Parade. LIEUT. TIDLER M.C. left to join 66th Division.	W.S.B.
	27th		Capt. MURGATROYD M.C. rejoined from Army Rest Station. Training in Physical drill, musketry, bombing and infantry drill. CAPT. SINGTON left Battalion to join 66th Division. Working.	W.S.B. W.S.B.
	28th		Party supplied for BAYENCOURT SWITCH. Working parties and training as above. Companies holding at ____	W.S.B. W.S.B.

WAR DIARY of 1/7th Bn. LANCASHIRE FUSILIERS

INTELLIGENCE SUMMARY

(Erase heading not required.)

Instructions regarding War Diaries and Intelligence Summaries are contained in F.S. Regs., Part II. and the Staff Manual respectively. Title pages will be prepared in manuscript.

Army Form C. 2118.

Place	Date	Hour	Summary of Events and Information	Remarks and references to Appendices
FRANCE Sheet. SYDNEY Bn. HQ. 77a 21.7.5	MAY. 29th		Training in Physical drill, bayonet fighting, musketry, and bombing. Companies bathed at Couin. One Company outfits working party.	w.P.B.
	30th		Practice attack by the companies at which Divisional General was present. Presentation of medal ribbons by Divisional General.	w.P.B.
	31st		Training as above. Strength of Battalion 31 Officers 485 other ranks.	w.P.B.

J Murphy Major
Cmdg. 1/7 Lan. Fus.

CONFIDENTIAL 125/4/2

WAR DIARY
11th BATTN.
LANCASHIRE FUSILIERS.
JUNE 1918

VOL 4

WAR DIARY of 1/4th LANCASHIRE FUSILIERS
or
INTELLIGENCE SUMMARY.

Army Form C. 2118.

(Erase heading not required).

Place	Date	Hour	Summary of Events and Information	Remarks and references to Appendices
FRANCE Ref Sheet 57dNE Bn HQ J26a 25/45	JUNE 1st		One company working on BAYENCOURT SWITCH. Remainder carried out scheme "Enveloping fire and movement on losing barrage" Church Parade. Musketry. Capt. P.A. SHEPHERDINE left battalion to be attached to 42nd Divisional Signal School.	W @/3
	2nd		Working parties and Coy schemes as above. Practice Signal Battle Positions.	W @/3
	3rd			W @/3
	4th		Working parties and training as above.	W @/3
	5th		Working parties and training as above.	W @/3
	6th		Working parties and training as above.	W @/3
Bn. HQ J3 & 45.40	7th		Moved from COUIN to ROSSIGNOL FARM.	W @/3
	8th		Training in Musketry and bombing.	W @/3
	9th		Church Parade, Musketry. 2/Lieut ELLIOT awarded D.S.O.	W @/3
	10th		Bombing, Physical drill, musketry and Infantry training. Enemy sent one H.V. shrapnel shell (about 15"inch) over camp. Two casualties. Lieut. Col BREWIS D.S.O. rejoined battalion from leave.	W @/3
	11th		Training as above. 2/Lieut KERR rejoined battalion from hospital.	W @/3
	12th		Training as above.	W @/3
Bn HQ J20c 94	13th		Battalion moved into wood at BUS.	W @/3

WAR DIARY OF 7th LANCASHIRE FUSILIERS.
INTELLIGENCE SUMMARY.
(Erase heading not required.)

Army Form C. 2118.

Instructions regarding War Diaries and Intelligence Summaries are contained in F.S. Regs. Part II. and the Staff Manual respectively. Title pages will be prepared in manuscript.

Place	Date	Hour	Summary of Events and Information	Remarks and references to Appendices
FRANCE Sheet 57dNE K.9a.10.20. Bn H.Q K.9a.10.20.	June 14th		Relieved 1/14th MANCHESTERS in line at HEBUTERNE. LIEUT WEBB rejoined Battalion from ENGLAND. 2/LIEUT WOOD rejoined from course	W.S.P.13.
	15th		1/14th MANCHESTERS raided FUSILIER TRENCH and got one prisoner. Casualties in Battalion 2 officers & 62 other ranks. Strength	W.S.P.B.
	16th		All men working in trenches during night. Patrol under LIEUT RIPPIGER was bombed by the enemy near FUSILIER TRENCH. Casualties 3.	W.S.P.13.
	17th		Enemy artillery active. HEBUTERNE SWITCH shelled at "stand to". Casualties 1 killed 3 wounded	W.S.P.13.
	18th		Enemy quiet. Bn H.Q. shelled. ~~Probably retaliation for raid on night of 17th by 5th EAST LANCS~~ WEBB. Casualties 1 wounded.	W.S.P.R.
	19th		Enemy quiet. Casualties nil	W.S.P.13
	20th		Quiet. Casualties nil	W.S.P.13
	21st		B Coy. H.Q. shelled twice with 5.9's. Casualties nil	W.S.P.13 W.S.P.13
	22nd		Getting Catacombs ready to be used as Bn. H.Q. Casualties nil	W.S.P.13
Bn H.Q. K.9a.60.70.	23rd		Relieved by 8th LANCASHIRE FUSILIERS and went into support	W.S.P.13
	24th		Enemy machine dropped bomb on A. Coy. H.Q. Casualties 1 wounded. Enemy artillery active. A. Coy. fairly well shelled. Two bombs dropped at B Coy. H.Q.	W.S.P.13.
	25th		Quiet. HEBUTERNE shelled frequently during day	W.S.P.13

WAR DIARY OF 7th LANCASHIRE FUSILIERS.

INTELLIGENCE SUMMARY.

Army Form C. 2118.

(Erase heading not required.)

Instructions regarding War Diaries and Intelligence Summaries are contained in F. S. Regs., Part II. and the Staff Manual respectively. Title pages will be prepared in manuscript.

Place	Date	Hour	Summary of Events and Information	Remarks and references to Appendices
FRANCE Sheet 57ᴰ N.E. Bn. H.Q. K9a60.90	June 26th		Naval artillery active. SAILLY – FON QUEVILLERS road shelled at intervals day	Casualties Nil
	27th		ROSSIGNOL WOOD very heavily shelled all day. Battalion on working parties. Casualties nil.	W.Q.R.
	28th		Working parties.	W.Q.R.
	29th		Quiet.	W.Q.R.
	30th		Enemy aircraft active during morning. Working parties. Casualties nil. Strength 42 officers, 890 other ranks.	W.Q.R.

1/7/18.

G.J.Bevan Lt.Col
c/o 7/7 Lancs. Fus
Fusiliers

CONFIDENTIAL

WAR DIARY

of

1/7th Bn. LAN. FUS

1st – 31st July 1918.

Volume 48.

WAR DIARY of 1/7th Bn LANCASHIRE FUSILIERS
or
INTELLIGENCE SUMMARY.

Army Form C. 2118.

(Erase heading not required.)

Instructions regarding War Diaries and Intelligence Summaries are contained in F. S. Regs., Part II. and the Staff Manual respectively. Title pages will be prepared in manuscript.

Place	Date	Hour	Summary of Events and Information	Remarks and references to Appendices
FRANCE Sheet 57D	JULY 1		Fairly quiet day, a few HEAVIES were dropped near Bn HQ. LT. E.B. WEBB and 4 O.R's bombed enemy front at K.16.d.4.2. Our casualties 2.	
Bn H.Q. at J.34.L.2.6.	2		Relieved by N.Z. R.B. marched via COURCELLES to DIVISIONAL RESERVE LINE behind COLINCAMPS. Bn HQ at J.34.L.2.6.	
	3		MAJOR A. HODGE D.S.O. M.C. 117th Bn MANCHESTER REGT. joined the BATTN. A B & C Coys supplied WORKING PARTIES.	
	4		LT.COL G.S. BREWIS D.S.O. took command of the 125 INF. BDE. in the absence of the BRIGADIER GENERAL. MAJOR A. HODGE D.S.O. M.C. took command of the BATTN. BATTLE SURPLUS rejoined from HALLOY.	
	5		All Coys supplied WORKING PARTIES and went to the BATHS at BERTRANCOURT. DRAFT arrived. 2nd LT. H.L. LAKEMAN rejoined the BATTN. from Hospital 2nd LT. J.E. ASHWORTH proceeded to 125 INF. BDE as BDE GAS OFFICER.	
	6		B & C Coys went to the BATHS at BERTRANCOURT. A & D Coys found WORKING PARTIES.	
	7		All Coys found WORKING PARTIES. Remainder in training on the range, remaining training in MUSKETRY & GAS DRILL.	

WAR DIARY of 1/7th BN LANCASHIRE FUSILIERS
or
INTELLIGENCE SUMMARY.
(Erase heading not required.)

Army Form C. 2118.

Place	Date	Hour	Summary of Events and Information	Remarks and references to Appendices
FRANCE Chalk Pit	JULY 8		Same as previous day.	MM
	9		All Coys found WORKING PARTIES, firing arms on the range, remained training	MM
			A BOCHE AEROPLANE brought down a BALLOON at BUS and escaped although damaged but flying low/land.	MM
BN.H.Q. at CHALK PIT K32 a.2.5.	10		Relieved 1/5th MANCHESTER REGT in the FRONT LINE. B Coy in FRONT LINE. C Coy in SUPPORT, A Coy at the APPLE TREES, D Coy in RESERVE.	MM
	11		FRONT LINE Milked by I.M's	MM
	12		A BOCHE AEROPLANE flew over BN. HQ @ Aeroplane escaped Chay aged at Road 4.339	MM
	13		D Coy was shelled rather heavily with 77mms, SUGAR FACTORY shelled with 5.9s	MM
	14		C & D Coys were shelled with 4.5's and whizzbangs for 40 minutes, A+D 2045	MM
	15		found WORKING PARTIES, FRONT LINE TRENCHES retained. A & D Coys found WORKING PARTIES, FRONT LINE TRENCHES retained. Strength of the BATT'N 42 OFFS & 943 O.R.s, Ration strength 24 OFFS & 640 ORs	MM
	16		Preparing for reconnaissance for bombardment, PATROLS sent out to reconnre.	MM
	17		In a raid operation B Coy captured. 1 PRISONER, 4 M.Ms awarded for the enterprise.	MM

WAR DIARY or INTELLIGENCE SUMMARY.

Army Form C. 2118.

of 1/7BN LANCASHIRE FUSILIERS.

(Erase heading not required.)

Place	Date	Hour	Summary of Events and Information	Remarks and references to Appendices
FRANCE	JULY			
About S.7D	18		C.Coy relieved B.Coy in FRONT LINE, A.COY in SUPPORT, B.Coy at the APPLETREES, D.Coy in RESERVE.	MM
	19		LT COL C.S. BREWIS D.S.O. took over command of the BATTN. 2nd LT W.M. McCREADY proceeded on leave to UK	MM
	20		A good PATROL was done by 2LT. W.H. BEECROFT, 6th GLOS. REGT.	MM
	21		C.Coy was shelled with 77 MMS from 5-0PM to 6-0PM.	MM
	22		C.Coy tried to take WATLING STREET in the afternoon, but failed. Casualties, 2LT J.W. WOOD WEST RIDING REGT. Wounded 2nd LT J.S. THOMSON WEST RIDING REGT. killed, 2nd LT W.H. BEECROFT, 6th GLOS REGT. killed & 34 O.R.S casualties.	MM
	23		Very quiet day except for a little shelling near B.H.Q	MM
	24		WATLING STREET was front area for 2 hours with HEAVIES. C.Coy sent out 3 PATROLS, PTE HEARDLEY M.M. reported laying out his pat.rol pulled 12 BOCHG	
			Our casualties 7 O.R.S., 2nd LT. W.H. BEECROFT down at BERTRAUCOURT in the BRITISH CEMETHRY.	MM
	25		We extremely weather wet.	MM
B~HQ at J34,B.2.6	26		Relieved by 1/5 4 BN EAST LANCASHIRE REGT and marched to the WINDMILL at J34,B.2.6 into DIVISIONAL RESERVE, B & C COYS in the PURPLE RESERVE LINE.	MM

WAR DIARY of 1/7th Bn. LANCASHIRE FUSILIERS.
or
INTELLIGENCE SUMMARY.

Army Form C. 2118.

(Erase heading not required.)

Place	Date	Hour	Summary of Events and Information	Remarks and references to Appendices
FRANCE	July			
Mailly-Maillet	26		A & D Coys in BERTRANCOURT. BATTLE SURPLUS rejoined. Took over the RESERVE LINE from the 1/10th BN MANCHESTER REGT.	
	27		BATT'N went to the BATHS at BERTRANCOURT. All Coys found WORKING PARTIES. Remainder training.	
	28		All Coys found WORKING PARTIES. Church parade at BERTRANCOURT. D Coy on the Rifle & Lewis gun Ranges.	
	29		Recruit DRAFTS inspected by the C.O. Remainder of Coys went to the BATHS at BERTRANCOURT. A Coy on the Rifle & Lewis of gun Ranges. Working Parties same as previous day.	
	30		2nd LT J.S. THOMSON buried at BERTRANCOURT in the BRITISH CEMETARY. D Coy on the Rifle & Lewis of gun Ranges. Working Parties same as previous day.	
	31		A & D Coys relieved B & C Coys in the PURPLE RESERVE LINE. Preparations for MINDEN DAY. Working Parties same as previous day. Nominal strength of BATT'N 40 OFFS. + 927 O.R's. Ration Strength 27 OFFS + 983 O.R's. 10 Officers + 16 N.C.O's attached a lecture on TANKS at BUS.	

G.S. Brero Lt. Col
Comdg 1/7 Lancs Fus.

WAR DIARY 88.6

1/7 LANCASHIRE FUSILIERS

AUGUST 1918

VOL 48

WAR DIARY of 1/1/7 Lan Fus
or INTELLIGENCE SUMMARY
(Erase heading not required.)

Army Form C. 2118.

Place	Date	Hour	Summary of Events and Information	Remarks and references to Appendices
BERTRANCOURT 57D T33	Aug 1		MINDEN DAY. B Coy & Hq details marched to Bus-les-Artois and were inspected by and inspected by	
			Past the Maj-Gen, who presented Cpl LEWIS, Pt RYLAND, Pte ROGERS with MM.	PAS
	2		Wet day. All coys found working parties, remainder training. Cpl McGOULD proceeded on	
			leave to UK. Lt. A.F. WORDEN took command of D Coy.	PAS
Toutel	3		Marched to COURCELLES & relieved 15 Man. Regt. in effect matters. Maj. HODGE DSO	
			in command. Lt Col BREWIS DSO at transport lines. Dispositions A Coy K14 & K19a	
			B Coy K15d & K14c. C Coy Foot Stagg at D Coy Taud r Bot.	PAS
	4		Capt A.W. BOYD MC reported from UK & took command of D Coy. Le Sigrry Farm	
			shelled with 59p.	PAS
	5		Capt B. SHELMERDINE went to division. 4 Casualties in D Coy.	PAS
	6		2/Lt T.R. GARBETT awarded MC. 4681 MYERSCOUGH awarded MM.	PAS
	7		Quiet day. Enemy shelled COINCAMPS & SHILLY-AU-BOIS at intervals. BRIG-GEN FARGUS CMG DSO	
			inspected company areas.	PAS
	8		Quiet day. A few fair shells fell during night in D Coy area.	PAS
	9		Lt Col BREWIS took over command. OC Coys reconnot'd front line LOby	
			5 LF. D Coy shelled rather heavily at intervals. Capt A.W. BOYD MC wounded.	PAS

WAR DIARY 1/7 Lan Fus

INTELLIGENCE SUMMARY

Army Form C. 2118.

Place	Date	Hour	Summary of Events and Information	Remarks and references to Appendices
Tap	Ag 10		Enemy aircraft active. 5 casualties in D Coy. PAS	
K26C1520	11		Relieved 1/5 LF. Batt Hq K26C1520. A & D Coy in line B Coy in support, C Coy in reserve. PAS	
	12		2/Lt. Climie sick to hospital. Enemy shelled HQ. A & B Coy area shelled heavily at stand to for 40 mins. 5 casualties. PAS	
	13		2/Lt. D W Chastney rejoined from Lewis Gun Course. Took command of D Coy. Div 2 Bde Commander visited line. PAS	
	14		Enemy retired from his front line behind SERRE. A & D Coy sent out patrols to front in front of SERRE and established posts. C Coy relieves A & D Patrols in WALTER Trench. B Coy formed a support line. Casualties 2. PAS	
	15		Coy patrols reconnoitred the ground through SERRE to first objective at K25d00 to K15b3550 then to second objective K26c20 & K26c53. A Coy relieves patrol at 1st & 2nd objective. Casualties 4. PAS	
	16		Enemy attacked 2 of our posts but were driven off from one. Enemy shelled SERRE, SERRE Ridge heavily. Lt. A.F. Worden proceeded on leave to UK. Capt E.C. Singleton rejoined from leave. Capt P.E. Brierley wounded. Casualties 4. PAS	

WAR DIARY of 17 LAN F. 3

INTELLIGENCE SUMMARY.

Place	Date	Hour	Summary of Events and Information	Remarks and references to Appendices
57D. Toufs	Aug 17		Div Bde Commander visited the front Coys. D Coy relieved A in front line. Relieved O in support. PMS	
	18		Enemy attacked our left post but was driven off. He then attacked our right post. 2/Lt P.C. KERR Killed. Casualton 6 missing. Other Prisoners. PMS	
	19		MAJ RACADE proceeded on leave to UK. PMS Capt PAYNE proceeded on leave to UK. SERRE heavily shelled during afternoon. Own patrols active. PMS	
	20		Hand 3rd Army was to attack from ARRAS southward. Objective for us BEAUREGARD DOVECOTE. Very quiet day. PMS 57D L29 L2691	
	21		Left FORT STEWART at 2.30 AM A+B Coys formed up West of broad gauge railway. A on left B on right at 2 o'clock they moved into position and at Zero + 2 hours moved forward to take up position behind 2nd objective reached by 5/LF. 5/LF reached objective + 7/LF then went through and reached 3rd objective with exception of DOVECOTE which was taken by A Coy at 2 AM following day. Capt SAUNDERS wounded. PMS by at K36a 66	
57D K36 b.6.	22		At 4.45 AM Enemy Counter attacked and our troops fell back with heavy casualties.	

Army Form C. 2118.

WAR DIARY of 1/7 LAN FUS
or
INTELLIGENCE SUMMARY.
(Erase heading not required.)

Place	Date	Hour	Summary of Events and Information	Remarks and references to Appendices
5/8 L25a 9.3			The fire flanks from the offside hill severed us to take up new position slightly in rear of our forward area on the north side of the wooded road. (57A L.27 28c) More prisoners taken. 2Lt H LAKEMAN killed. Bn. Hq. at L25a 9.3.	PKS
	Aug 23		Came out of line having been engaged at by H.E. on our flanks. The line having taken a right turn to our original frontage. Btn Comp in Observation Wood. Batt Hq. at K21c 65.70	PKS
			A.B.D.Coys at huts at COURCELLES. Batt moved to WALTER TRENCH Hq. at K29d 60 95.	PKS
K29d 60 95	Aug 24		Moved to MIRAUMONT 7.15pm by road. Bivouacked North of Town. Hq. L37 central Arrived about 9.45pm in a thunderstorm. Made shelters	PKS
13A central	Aug 25		Continued making bivouacks	PKS
	Aug 26		Moved to Pys arriving 10.6 pm. Hq. in sunken road M2180. Coys all clear.	PKS
5/c M2180	Aug 27		Reconnoitred reference positions near WARLENCOURT (M10) & route to GREVILLERS	PKS
	Aug 28		Commenced to prepare defensive positions near WARLENCOURT when orders were given to return to camp & prepare to move forward. Railway was reformed. Did not move (Everything was postponed in real haste	PKS

Army Form C. 2118.

WAR DIARY of 1/7 Lan Fus
or
INTELLIGENCE SUMMARY.

(Erase heading not required.)

Place	Date	Hour	Summary of Events and Information	Remarks and references to Appendices
S14 M31 80	Aug 30		In readiness to move all day, but no orders to move received. PAS	
	31		Bn. moved into support from reserve in afternoon. Bn. relieved 1/5 East Lancs at LE BARQUE, arriving 4.15 pm. Headquarters at M15 d 8.4 in old enemy camp. Coys all in close proximity. Defensive positions reconnoitred by Coy Commanders in evening. PAS	
M15 d 8.4				

E.J. Shira, Lieut Colonel
Commdg. 1/7 Born Fus.

2/9/18

WAR DIARY

VOL. 50.

7th BATTN. LAN FUS.

1 – 30th SEPTEMBER. 1918.

Army Form C. 2118.

WAR DIARY
or
INTELLIGENCE SUMMARY.

of 1/1st LANCASHIRE FUSILIERS.

(Erase heading not required.)

Instructions regarding War Diaries and Intelligence Summaries are contained in F. S. Regs., Part II. and the Staff Manual respectively. Title pages will be prepared in manuscript.

Place	Date	Hour	Summary of Events and Information	Remarks and references to Appendices
Bn H.Q. at	Mar 1st		Major A. HODGE, D.S.O, M.C. took over command of the 1/5" MANCHESTER REGT.	
			All Coys training in Lewis gun & Musketry.	
			2/Lt J.K. ALLISON, 2/LT W. ELLIS, & 2/LT H.T. DOWNHAM joined the Battn from England.	MM
	2nd		All Coys training in Lewis Gun & Musketry.	MM
			Lieut W.T. O'BRYEN M.C. proceeded on leave to U.K.	MM
	3rd	9-AM	The Battn marched to RIENCOURT & took up a defensive position. A & B Coys in front line, C & D Coys formed a flank position.	MM
B.H.Q. at		4-30 P.M	At 4-30 P.M the Battn marched to BARASTRE via VILLERS-au-FLOS & thence the night there. Defensive positions were reconnoitred EAST of BUS.	MM
0.15.B.2.6			At B & C Coys took up a defensive position east of BUS. in O.24.B&d.	MM
B.H.Q. at	4		D Coy in support in BUS.	
O.23.d.5.7		11-30AM	B.C & D Coys moved to the RAILWAY EMBANKMENT in P.19.t.d Enemy put over a good number of GAS SHELLS during the day.	MM
			2/Lt WALFORD proceeded on leave to U.K.	MM

WAR DIARY of 1/4 & 1/3 Lancashire Fusiliers

or INTELLIGENCE SUMMARY.

Army Form C. 2118.

(Erase heading not required.)

Place	Date	Hour	Summary of Events and Information	Remarks and references to Appendices
Sheet 57cSE	date 5th		D Company was ordered to attack a line of trenches east of NEUVILLE BOITON VAL	
			running from P.23 d.06 to P.29 L 27	
		4-30 pm	D Coy formed up in the main road in NEUVILLE (P22d 15.60 to P.13a 15.35)	
		5-30 pm	A creeping barrage was put down in P.23 a 1 C & a stationary barrage on the objective	
			The creeping barrage advanced 100 yds every 3 minutes until the objective was	
			taken, then a standing barrage was put down on P.23 a 26 to P.29 a 37 for 15 minutes	
		5-42 P.M.	D Coy started to advance to their objective (P.23 d 06 to P.29 L 27), the left platoon	
			got on their objective at P.23 a 85.60, however on 3 moving platoons were held up by	
			heavy M.G. fire in P.23 C 73 + P.29 a 79. 102 prisoners were captured including 6 officers	
Sheet 57c S.W. Batta H.Q at M.20 c79			Advanced Battn H.Q at P.19 a 25. A General Robert Batta was established at P.15 d S.G.	
		3-30am	The Battn was relieved by the 2nd NEW ZEALAND Bde & came back in to reserve on	
			P4s by motor lorry. All casualties Lt R.E. SMALE & 2/Lt W ELLIS wounded	
			3 O.R's killed & 14 O.R's wounded.	
			MAJOR L. EDGE rejoined the Battn from 125 INF 3 DE.	
			Capt. B. A. PAYNE rejoined the Battn from leave from U.K.	WMP

WAR DIARY
or
INTELLIGENCE SUMMARY.

Army Form C. 2118.

Place	Date	Hour	Summary of Events and Information	Remarks and references to Appendices
Montigny S. Mat	6th		The Battalion spent the day cleaning up & fitting. Battalion Drills resumed.	
			2/Lt. T.M. McCREADY rejoined the Battn. from 42nd Div. LEWIS GUN SCHOOL.	Appx
	7th		2/Lt. T. COOLE, 2/Lt. F. WOOD & 2/Lt. H.T. WARREN joined the Battn. from England.	Appx
			The day was spent in bathing and cleaning up. Lt. H.T.A. RIPPERGER proceeded on leave to U.K.	Appx
	8th		A Brigade Church parade was held near P.F.S. & Coy at the trotts.	Appx
	9th		2/Lt. G.D. THORP rejoined the Battn. from leave from U.K.	Appx
			A demonstration by the R.S.M. "Locking in" by the Brown. H.Q. & Coy at the trotts.	
			The Battn. had their gas helmets tested. 2/Lt. W.G. BROWN rejoined the Battn. from a signal course.	Appx
	10th		All Coys training in Musketry + 10 rounds Rapid. 2/Lt. T.M. McCREADY formed a Brigade Lewis Gun School. Very heavy rain during the day.	Appx
			All Coys Musketry in Lewis Gun & Musketry + 10 rounds Rapid. D. Coy at the trotts.	
	11th		2/Lt. T.M. CLINIE rejoined the Battn. from hospital. Very heavy rain during the day.	Appx

WAR DIARY of 7th Bn Royal Inniskilling Fusiliers

Army Form C. 2118.

INTELLIGENCE SUMMARY.
(Erase heading not required.)

Place	Date	Hour	Summary of Events and Information	Remarks and references to Appendices
Sheet 57°S.W. Bn H.Q. at M.2.d.79	12th		A&B Coys went for route march. H.Q. C&D Coys at the baths.	
	13th		A&B Coys innoculated. 2/Lt W.G. BROWN proceeded on leave to U.K.	
			A&C Coys practised an attack scheme. B&D Coys training on the range.	
			C&D Coys innoculated	
	14th		B&D Coys practised an attack scheme. A&C Coys training on the range.	
	15th		Coys proceeded to WARLENCOURT where clothes were disinfected.	
	16th		2/Lt W. PROCTOR proceeded on leave to U.K. Strength of Battn 44 Officers 784 O.R.'s	
			A&C Coys practised an attack scheme. 1 section of 42 M.G.Bn & 1 section of 125 T.M.B co-operated in the scheme. B Coy training on the range. D Coy building a new rifle range	
	17th		The Battn proceeded to a TANK DEMONSTRATION at IRLES, at very heavy storm during the night. H.Q. C&D Coys at the baths.	
	18th		B&D Coys practised an attack scheme. 1 section of 42 M.G.Bn & 1 section of 125 T.M.B co-operated in the scheme. A&C Coys on the range, and at the baths.	
			CAPT. E.C. SINGTON proceeded on leave to U.K.	

WAR DIARY of 7th Bn Lancashire Fusiliers

INTELLIGENCE SUMMARY
(Erase heading not required.)

Army Form C. 2118.

Place	Date	Hour	Summary of Events and Information	Remarks and references to Appendices
Sheet 57C S.W. Edn E.				
Bn H.Q at M2 d.7.9	19th		B & D Coys practised an attack scheme. 1 section of 42 M.G. Bn + 1 section of 125 T.M.B. co-operated in the scheme. A & C Coys on the range.	MM
	20th		A & C Coys practised a combined attack scheme with M.G & T.M. sections attached. B & D Coys training on the range. C & D Coys at the baths. 2/Lt. E.W. CHASTNEY proceeded on leave to U.K.	MM
	21st		A & C Coys practised an attack scheme. 1 section of 42nd M.G. Bn & 1 section of 125 T.M.B. co-operated in the scheme. B & D Coys training on the range. Rest of the day spent preparing for the move. Battle Surplus handed to DIVISIONAL RECEPTION CAMP at MIRAUMONT. Lieut W.T. O'BRYEN rejoined the Battn from leave.	MM
Sheet 57M N.W. Bn H.Q at I 30 a 9.8.	22nd		The Battn marched from CYS to LEBUCQUIERE via WARLENCOURT - BAPAUME - FREMICOURT into Divisional Reserve.	MM
	23rd		Fatigue Parties improving billets. Coys training in Lewis gun. HAVRINCOURT WOOD reconnoitred. CAPT R.R. BREWIS M.C. proceeded on leave to U.K.	MM
	24th		Fatigue Parties improving billets. H.Q & A Coys at the baths at VELU. 2/Lt WALFORD rejoined the Battn from leave.	MM

WAR DIARY of 7th Bn Lancashire Fusiliers   Army Form C. 2118.
or
INTELLIGENCE SUMMARY.

Place	Date	Hour	Summary of Events and Information	Remarks and references to Appendices
Must 5° N.W. Lept				
Bn H.Q. at 2.5"			Fatigue parties unloading SHELLS. Leave from Training. B, C & D Coys at the Baths.	
I 30 a 9.8.			CAPT. P.E. BRIERLEY rejoined the Battn. from Hospital. LT. R.T.A. RIPPERGER rejoined from leave. CAPT. F.W. COLLEY proceeded on leave to U.K.	YMM
Batt H.Q. at	26th		The Battn. entrained at LEBUCQUIERE & detrained at RUYAULCOURT & marched into	
Q 10 b 76			assembly positions through HAVRINCOURT WOOD. A Coy in BONES ALLEY, B Coy in SHERWOOD AVENUE & Trench running to DERBY RESERVE, C Coy in SNAP TRENCH, D Coy in SHERWOOD AVENUE, 2/Lt T.M. CLIMIE proceeded on leave to U.K.	YMM
	27th	8-2AM	A Coy attached took the 1st Objective (QSd 6527 to Q11d 9055) and at 8-35 AM B Coy the 2nd M.I. leapfrogging them advanced to 2nd Objective (Q6C 9027 to Q12 b 309) but were held up at Q12 a 85 by M.G's firing from their right flank from either in or near BEAUCAMP about Q12 a 94 which had been reported cleared.	
		9-30AM	The front was practically the same C Coy having advanced to help B Coy on the right, D Coy being part in front of 1st Objective waiting till they advanced.	
		9-45AM	B Coy reported they were at Q12 a 6555 & enemy were counter attacking at Q12 a 93	

WAR DIARY 7th Bn Lancashire Fusiliers
INTELLIGENCE SUMMARY
Army Form C. 2118.

Place	Date	Hour	Summary of Events and Information	Remarks and references to Appendices
HULLUCH	July 27th		Enemy attempted to break up BEAUCHAMP SUPPORT but were driven off	
		11·40AM/11·11PM	C.Coy had to withdraw to 1st Objective owing to our own barrage of W. How. which	See HHI
		11-15PM	was firing on M. in Neuts. A TANK was seen working round N. of BEAUCHAMP but was put out of action	
		1·20PM	C. Coy reported they had reached Q.12.a.5.0.0 but were held up by machine gun fire from near tank at Q.12.a.7.2 and they were attempting to out flank this attack this was not successful.	
		3·0PM	Enemy were seen in BEAUCHAMP trying to work round our right flank but were stopped by C. Coy. A patrol was then sent in co-operation with the 5th DIVISION to work round the north end of BEAUCHAMP to attack the M.G. Nests in flank. Orders were received (that a general attack (5th DIVISION 7th & 8th L.F.) with a barrage would take place at 6·30PM this was put off till the morning of the 28th. Total number of prisoners captured 120. Casualties, LIEUT A.S. TENNANT killed MAJOR R.H. CADE & CAPT. H.L. MURGATROYD died of wounds. LIEUT. S. AUSTIN, 2/LT. A.J. DOWNHAM, 2/LT. W. STEELE, 2/LT. J.K. ALLISON, 2/LT. A.J. WARREN & 2/LT. F.L. WALFORD wounded.	WM

WAR DIARY 7th Bn Lancashire Fusiliers

Army Form C. 2118.

WAR DIARY
or
INTELLIGENCE SUMMARY.
(Erase heading not required.)

Place	Date	Hour	Summary of Events and Information	Remarks and references to Appendices
Hart of 7th Bn fus	28th	2.30 AM	D. Coy attached the BROWN LINE (2nd Objective) under a rolling barrage & captured and 200 prisoners. LT AUSTIN & 2/LT A.J. DUNHAM died of wounds.	
Batt. HQ	29th		The 1st NEW ZEALAND BRIGADE went through the BROWN LINE & the Battn came	
at Q6a27			back into reserve in HAVRINCOURT WOOD (Q2). CAPT. R.A. SHELMERDINE reported	M.
			from 125 Bde. 2/LT W. STEELE died of wounds.	M.
	30th		All Coys recommencing training etc. 2/Lt W.G. BROWN rejoined from leave.	M.
			Strength of the Battn 36 Officers & 660 O.R's.	M.

G.S. Bruin Lt. Col.
Cdg. 7th Bn Lancashire Fusiliers

App.I

SECRET.

ADDITION No.1. to 7TH.LAN.FUS. OPERATION ORDER No.65.   26/9/18.

1. The Battalion will proceed from the Debussing Point by Route March via MATHESON ROAD and CLAYTON CROSS to Q15a.1.9. where there will be guides from the 126th.Infantry Brigade. Intervals of 200 yards to be maintained between platoons.

2. A WATER DUMP will be formed at this point under SGT.PRICE, each Company dumping 10 Petrol Tins there.

3. LEWIS GUNS will be picked up at this point and carried forward to the assembly trenches as follows :-
   A. Coy........ SHERWOOD AVENUE clear of Barrage line.
   B. Coy........ SLIP TRENCH running N. out of SHERWOOD AVENUE.
   C. Coy........ SNAP TRENCH.
   D. Coy........ SHERWOOD AVENUE W. of Trench junction Q11.a.2.5.
   Hd.Qrs....... Q10.b.83.

4. Reference Table "A" and map already issued :-
   A. Coy. will attack 1st. Objective.
   B. Coy. will attack 2nd. Objective.
   C. Coy. will attack 3rd. Objective.
   D. Coy. will attack 4th. Objective:
   each Company leap-frogging the other.

5. Each company as it takes its objective will establish a Relay Runner Post in the centre of the objective taken, so that the Forward Coy. Runners can use these Posts as Relay Posts.

6. All Companies will go in with Waterbottles filled, and Rations for the 28th. inst. in addition to Iron Rations.
   27

7. Each man will be provided with 2 No.36 Grenades, to be used either with Cup Discharger or as a hand grenade.

8. 24.Discs per Company have been issued for use with Contact Aeroplane.

9. D.Company will carry 24.S.O.S.Rockets and 50 Very Lights.

10. AMENDMENT TO OPERATION ORDER NO.65.
    For S.W. corner of HAVRINCOURT WOOD read RUYAULCOURT.
    For embuss at 3:0.p.m. read not embuss till after 6:0.p.m.

Distribution as for O.O.65.

A. Debruham
Capt. & Adjt.,
7th.Lancashire Fusiliers.

SECRET. 7TH. LANCASHIRE FUSILIERS OPERATION ORDER. No.65.

26/9/18.

Refce. Map Sheet 57.c.N.E. & S.E.

1. The IV Corps will attack BEAUCAMP RIDGE and HIGHLAND RIDGE and is to clear the HINDENBURG LINE as far as the GOUILLEN VALLEY. If the advance of the VI Corps on MASNIERES is successful the IV Corps is to advance to WELSH RIDGE to cover the flank of the VI Corps.

2. The attack on the 42nd Divisional Front will be carried out by the 126th Infantry Brigade on the Right, and the 127th Infantry Brigade on the Left.

3. The attack on the 126th Infantry Brigade Front will be carried out by the 7th Lan. Fus. on the Right and the 5th Lan. Fus. on the Left in accordance with Table "A".

4. On the night 26th/27th September, the 127th Infantry Brigade will withdraw from the line, leaving a screen of outposts to hold the line and to patrol the Divisional Front. Under cover of these outposts the 125th Infantry Brigade will move into their assembly positions in accordance with Table "B".

5. Two Tanks will be detailed by O.C. C.Coy. 11th Battn. Tanks, to deal with KILNER FARM and BOAR COPSE locality. All ranks will be made acquainted with the signals to be used between Tanks and Infantry.

6. The 59th Squadron R.A.F. are sending a Contact Aeroplane to call for flares at the following hours :-

    ZERO plus 220, on RED objective
    ZERO plus 300, on Brown and Brown dotted objectives.
    Zero plus 420, on Blue objective.

    In addition special reconnaissances have been arranged.
    The signal to denote the assembly of the enemy to counter-attack will be dropping of a RED Smoke Bomb over the place where the enemy is seen.
    Code Letters for communicating to the Plane will be the Four Letter Code Calls at present in use by the Division.

7. All troops are again to be warned against entering dug-outs before they have been examined, and passed as safe by R.E.

8. "Handshakes" have been arranged with the 18th. Infantry Brigade at the following points :-
    SUNKEN ROAD ..... BLACK Dotted Line.
    YORK AVENUE ..... RED LINE
    HIGHLAND ROAD.....BLUE Line.
    R.S.s.L.?.

9. Watches will be synchronised by an Officer of 125th. Infantry Brigade Headquarters at the Headquarters of Units on "Y" night.

10. ACKNOWLEDGE.

Issued by .... at ....

Capt. & Adjt.,
7th. Lancashire Fusiliers.

Copies to :-
No.1................ C.O.
No.2................ O.C. A. Coy.
No.3................ O.C. B. Coy.
No.4................ O.C. C. Coy.
No.5................ O.C. D. Coy.
No.6................ I.O.

TABLE "A" To accompany 7th. LAN. FUS. OPERATION ORDER No. 36.

NOTE. ZERO Hour is the hour at which the Corps to the North of us start their attack.

ZERO plus 152. — Initial Barrage commences and stands for 10 minutes.

ZERO plus 162. — Leading Companies of 7th. and 8th. Lan. Fus. advance to first objective under rolling barrage.

ZERO plus 182. — Barrage reaches protective line for 1st. objective and stands for 8 minutes.

ZERO plus 190. — Second Companies of 7th. and 8th. Lan. Fus. having leap-frogged leading companies, advance to 2nd. objective under rolling barrage, the company of the 8th. Lan. Fus. after reaching 2nd. Objective makes a swing pivoted on their Right and still under rolling barrage, so as to get on the BROWN Line; at the same time the first company of the 8th. Lan. Fus. swing pivoted on their right so as to get on line of road running North and South in Q.6.a & b. and in line with 1st. company of 7th. Lan. Fus.

ZERO plus 222 — Barrage reaches protective line for BROWN line and stands for 8 minutes.

ZERO plus 230 — Third Companies of 7th. Lan. Fus. and 8th. Lan. Fus. having leap-frogged second Companies in BROWN Line advance under rolling barrage to 3rd. Objective.
8th. Lan. Fus. occupy SNAP TRENCH, CHERWOOD AVENUE, BERRY Support, BERRY TRENCH, and southern portion of CHAPEL WOOD Switch.

ZERO plus 262. — Barrage reached protective line for 3rd. Objective and stands for 54 minutes.

ZERO plus 270 — Right Flank of 7th. Lan. Fus. Company in 3rd. Objective advances under rolling barrage to PLOUGH Trench to join up with 5th. Division on South.

ZERO plus 321 — Fourth Companies of 7th. and 8th. Lan. Fus. having leap-frogged third Companies, advance under rolling barrage to final objective.

ZERO plus 324. — Barrage reaches protective line on South.

ZERO plus 348. — Barrage reaches protective line on North.

Vol 21

CONFIDENTIAL

WAR
DIARY
VOL. 51.
7th BATT. LAN. FUS.
1 - 31 OCTOBER 1918.

40.L
14 sheets

WAR DIARY of 1/5 Bn Manchester Fusiliers Vol. 51

or

INTELLIGENCE SUMMARY.

Army Form C. 2118.

(Erase heading not required.)

Place	Date	Hour	Summary of Events and Information	Remarks and references to Appendices
FRANCE Hurtebise	Oct 1st		Coys reorganising & cleaning up. Shelters improved.	
Batt H.Q. at Q.5.a.8.2	2nd		A & D Coys at the butts at TRESCAULT. B & C Coys Training on the range. LT. W.F. O'BRYEN awarded a bar to his M.C. LT. R.T.A. RIPPERGER awarded the M.C.	
	3rd		CAPT. P.E. BRIERLEY rejoined the Battn from Battle Surplus. All Coys training in P.T., B.E., Musketry, Close Order Drill & Gas Drill. H. & C. Coys at the butts at TRESCAULT. 2/LT. I. KEMPTON joined the Battn from the Base.	
	4th		A & D Coys practiced an attack scheme. 1 section of 42nd M.G. Bn & 1 section of 125 T.M.B. co-operated in the scheme. B & C Coys training in Musketry, Close Order Drill & Gas Drill. LT. A.F. WORDEN & 2/LT. C.M. PEARSON awarded the M.C.	
	5th		B & C Coys practised an attack scheme. 1 section 42nd M.G. Bn & 1 section of 125 T.M.B. co-operated in the scheme. A & D Coys training in Musketry, Close Order Drill, Extended Order Drill & Gas Drill. D Coy at the butts.	
	6th		Church Parade in Y.M.C.A. Tent at Clayton Camp, HURINCOURT WOOD. All Coys on the range. MAJOR E. HORSFALL M.C. 1/8th MANCHESTER REGT. joined the Battn from England.	

WAR DIARY of 7th Bn. Lancashire Fusiliers

or

INTELLIGENCE SUMMARY.

Army Form C. 2118.

(Erase heading not required.)

Place	Date	Hour	Summary of Events and Information	Remarks and references to Appendices
Hond 57SE	Oct			
Batt H.Q. at	7th		The Battn practised an attack scheme for the Major-General, the rest of the day spent preparing for the move.	H.M.
Q8a82	8th		The Battn marched to VILLERS-PLOUICH via TRESCAULT & BEAUCAMP & bivouacked in the railway embankment.	H.M.
Batt HQ at R13d75				
Batt 57B T40000	9th		The Battn marched to LE BOSQUET via SONNET FARM, BONAVIS FARM & LES RUES des VIGNES, & rested for midday meal, then marched to ESNES via LESDAIN	H.M.
Batt HQ at N4a57			LE GRAND PONT. Billetted in empty houses.	
Butt H.Q at I15c94	10th		The Battn marched from ESNES to FONTAINE-au-PIRE via LONGSART. The Battn was billetted in empty houses. Red H.Q joined the Battn from HAVRINCOURT WOOD	H.M.
Batt HQ at J1a98	11th		The Battn marched from FONTAINE-au-PIRE to AUDICOURT FARM. LT. E.W.S. PINK rejoined the Battn from U.K. CAPT R.R. 13 REWIS M.C. & 2/LT. F.W. CHASTNEY rejoined from leave.	H.M.
Batt H.Q. at D2648J	12th		The Battn relieved the 2nd WELLINGTON REGT. in support. CAPT. P.A. SHELMERDINE took over 125 Bde signals.	H.M.

3.

WAR DIARY of 7th Bn Lancashire Fusiliers   Army Form C. 2118.

or

INTELLIGENCE SUMMARY.

(Erase heading not required.)

Place	Date	Hour	Summary of Events and Information	Remarks and references to Appendices
HUTMONT	Oct			
Batt. H.Q. at	13th		All Coys continuing training. LT. J.M. McCREADY rejoined from 42nd DIVISIONAL SCHOOL	MM.
D 26 a 7.3			GAS SCHOOL. CAPT. F.W. COLLEY rejoined from leave from U.K.	
	14th		All Coys training in an attack scheme. LT. G.D. THORP took over command of C Coy & 2/LT. F.W. CHASTNEY took over D Coy, CAPT. A.M.C. DEBENHAM proceeded on leave to U.K.	MM.
Batt. H.Q. at	15th		The Batt. relieved the 1/5 Bn LANCASHIRE FUSILIERS in the front line in front of BRIASTRE, C & D Coys in the front line, A & B Coys in support.	MM.
D 28 a 5.1			Strength 21 Officers & 478 O.R's	
	16th		C & D Coys holding the front line, A & B Coys in support. LT. H.M. GOULD M.C. & 2/LT. J.M. CLINIE rejoined from leave. D Coy established a new post in a FARM at E 9 a 3.6. A Coy were reorganised. Casualties 8	MM.
	17th		Front line Coys making fire steps. The enemy put down a heavy barrage on the Battery at D 28 c & d. Heavy shelling near Batt H.Q.s during the night. Casualty	MM.
Batt H.Q. at	18th		1/10 MANCHESTER REGT relieved the Batt. in the front line at BRIASTRE & Came into reserve at BEAUVOIS. CAPT. E.E. SINGTON rejoined from leave, the following	
I & C 12			Officers joined the Battn. from U.K. MAJOR W.H. LOWE, 20th L.F. CAPT. E. WILLIAMSON 2/LT H.J. CARTER, 2/LT. R. BATTY, & 2/LT. S.S. WRIGHT,	MM.

SECRET   MOWE OPERATION ORDER No 70
                                    12.10.17   Copy

(1) At Zero + 80 (approx) 13th inst, the Battn. will attack the Blue Line. On conclusion of this attack the 2nd N.Z. Inf Bde will go through the 125 Bde.

(2) In conjunction with troops on right and left, 125 Bde will resume the attack. 8th L.F. on left, 7th L.F. on right and 5th L.F. in support.

(3) Boundaries. As communicated to O.C. Coys today (inter Battn & inter Coy).

(4) The Battalion will form up in road running north and south through E.9.d and E.15.a and attack in North-Easterly direction under a creeping barrage pace 100 yds per 6 minutes passing through Green, Red, & Purple objectives, and capturing the Blue Line with Battn. boundaries as per map issued today.

(3)

2 platoons of B Coy attached.
D Coy will be on the left with 1
platoon of B Coy attached.
C Coy will be 100 yds in support - 1
platoon in support of A Coy, and
one platoon in support of D Coy.
These 2 platoons will advance as
far as black dotted line unless
asked to reinforce the forward Coys.

(5) Special Parties: 1 Platoon of B Coy
will mop up and consolidate at E10 Central.
1 Platoon of B Coy will mop up and
consolidate cross roads in vicinity of
Quarry in E10 d 87. The 2 platoons
will if necessary form a right defensive
flank.
1 platoon of B Coy on left will mop up
and consolidate cross roads in E 4 C.
The above 3 platoons under their
Officers will form the main system
of communication back to Battn H.Q.
especially the platoon in E 10 central
to which all messages will be sent
for transmission.

(3) Direction. All platoon and Coy Commanders will advance by the compass.

Flanks. Right & left flanks of the Bde will be indicated by artillery firing Thermite shells about 500 yds. in advance of our front troops.

A central Thermite beacon will be fired by igniting the stacks in cross roads in 4 b. This will indicate the centre of the Bde. front and will be used as a check to the compass bearing.

It will move forward 500 yds further EAST when we get to within 500 yards of it. Coys will pay the greatest attention to direction, as the barrage is falling in Echelon of the line.

Assembly Positions. A Coy will assemble on road E 15 Central to E 9 d & 0.

D Coy will assemble from E 9 d & 0 to cross roads E 9 d 2 9.

C Coy will assemble along bank of the Braid Brook in E 9 c and E 15 a.

(4) Outposts will go through and

(4)

forward of the Blue Line at Zero + 240 and will be withdrawn at 0800.

(e) SUPPORT BATTALION 2 Coys of the 5th L.F. will be in support to the Battalion and will move forward in rear of the Battn at 0220 hours, and occupy positions held by us into green dotted line and into Brown line. They will only be called upon in event of a counter-attack or help us if the attack is hung up, or form a defensive flank. If any of the above measures are necessary, application will be made to Battn H.Q.

(g) BARRAGE The attack will be supported by five brigades of artillery plus 42 Div L.T.M. battery forming a creeping barrage at rate of 100 yds per 6 minutes. The initial barrage will fall at zero + 80 from E 16 a 0.7 E 4 a 7)

3.O. Smoke shell will be fired to indicate the arrival of the

barrage on the Blue Line. Smoke shells will also be fired to screen the troops on the Blue Line after daylight, until the NZ's advance has passed them.
At 0825 hours a barrage will be put down 200 yds E. of Blue Line. At 0840 hours the barrage will lift and the 2nd N.Z. Inf. Bde. will advance.

(9) Machine Guns. 22 Machine Guns from C and D Coys of 4th M.G. Batt. are available for the purpose of consolidating the Blue Line, and also for covering the advance of the 2nd N.Z. Inf. Bde's when it goes forward.

(10) Trench Mortars. 125th L.T.M. Bty. is arranging for 6 guns to fire during the initial barrage as follows:-

A. Two guns from positions in E 9 b. to fire on targets at E 10 a.

B. 4 guns in E 3 b. are in to fire on cross roads in E 4 b.

ndshakes with the right flank will take place at the following points:-

(6)
(a) E 10 c 40
(b) E 10 central
(c) Road junction E 10 b 4.7
(d) E 5 c 6.6
   With Left Brigade :-
(a) E 3 d 8.5
(b) E 4 b 2.5
(c) E 4 b 5.5

(11) Signals. Signal arrangements are issued separately to the Signalling Officer.

(12) Hoist aeroplane will call for flares at 0700 hrs. Flares are being distributed tonight.

(13) Watches will be synchronised at 1900 hours tonight.

(14) Stripping post. A post of police and pioneers will be established at cross roads E 14 d 4.6. at 0800 hours.
     Men escorting down prisoners of war will hand them over and return immediately to their Coys.

(7)
(8) The Aid Post will be at Battn HQrs in Sunken Road at E14a 5.3.
(9) Reports will be sent to Battn. HQ Qrs in Sunken Road at E14 a 5.3.
ACKNOWLEDGE.

22.10.18

Capt & S/Adjt
M.C.W?

Army Form C. 2118.

WAR DIARY of 1/8th Lancashire Fusiliers
or
INTELLIGENCE SUMMARY.
(Erase heading not required.)

Place	Date	Hour	Summary of Events and Information	Remarks and references to Appendices
Hants St 1-4-B.O.O. Batt H.Q at	Oct 19		The Batt. marched from BEAUVOIS to AULCOURT FARM & took over from the 1/6"	WW
			MANCHESTER REGT.	
D25d 35	20th		Preparing to go into the line & relieve the 127th Bde. CAPT. W. KELLY rejoined the Battn.	WW
	21st		The Battn. relieved the 1/7th MANCHESTER REGT & 2 Coys of the 1/5th MANCHESTER	WW
Batt. HQ at			REGT. in the front line. A & B Coys in front line. C & D Coys in support.	
E14.a.4.2.	22nd		Preparing for the attack. MAJOR W.H. LOWE & 2/LT. J. KEMPTON wounded.	WW
			2/LT. H.T. CARTER killed. C. Coy were heavily shelled during the day.	
	23rd	0100	The Battn. formed up in the road running North & South through E9d & E15a.	
		0326	The attack was resumed by the 125" In.F. Bde. 7th LAN. FUS. on the right & 1/8"	see Appx.
			LAN. FUS. on the left & 1/5 " LAN. FUS. in support.	
			A & D Coys attacked & captured the 1st Objective. (green line E9.d.45.15 & E10.c.31)	
			& then went forward & captured the 2nd Objective. (Red line E.a.25.61. E.10.b.15.15)	
			On this Objective the fighting was anything but right-hand being held	
			up by a Nest of M.G.'s in E10.d. C Coy extended into dead ground	
			preparatory to outflanking the M.G.'s meanwhile two tanks arrived from	
			the left flank & proceeded to help in overcoming the M.G.'s	

WAR DIARY of 7th Bn. Lancashire Fusiliers

or
INTELLIGENCE SUMMARY.

(Erase heading not required.)

Army Form C. 2118.

Place	Date	Hour	Summary of Events and Information	Remarks and references to Appendices
Hunts 7B 140000	Oct 23rd		With the aid of the tanks, A Coy successfully got past the obstacle & captured the PURPLE LINE (E4 d 07 & E5 c 00) D Coy reached the PURPLE LINE meeting with very little resistance.	
		0740	A & D Coys left the PURPLE LINE & captured the FINAL OBJECTIVE (BLUE LINE W28 d 3) to E5c 7562) at 0733. C Coy mopped up the PURPLE LINE, B Coy mopped up the RED LINE, the QUARRY in E4d & CROSS ROADS in E4d. A Report Centre was established at E10 central.	
		0840	The 2nd NEW ZEALAND BDE. passed through the FINAL OBJECTIVE.	
		1200	The Battn. marched back to VIESLY. Casualties. LT. R.T.A. RIPPERGER MC & LT. E.W. SPINK killed. 2/LT. R. BATTY wounded. 12 O.R's killed, 6 F O.R's wounded to 15 O.R's missing.	WM
Bn. H.Q. at 24th			The Battn. marched from VIESLY to FONTAINE-au-PIRE into reserve.	
			MAJOR C. ALDERSON D.S.O, LT. D. McLACHLAN, 6th Bn. LAN. FUS. CAPT. WHAMOND YORK & LANCS REGT. joined the Battn. from England.	WM
I 15 a 71	25th		The day was spent in cleaning up & reorganising. LT. COL. T.J. KELLY M.C. 18th Bn. MANCHESTER REGT. joined the Battn and assumed command vice LT. COL. G.S. BREWIS D.S.O. WELSH REGT. to whom 2/LT. F. WOOD awarded the M.C.	WM

WAR DIARY of 7th Bn Lancashire Fusiliers

Army Form C. 2118.

or

INTELLIGENCE SUMMARY.

(Erase heading not required.)

Place	Date	Hour	Summary of Events and Information	Remarks and references to Appendices
About 57B I-40 a.o.o	Oct 26th		Corps training in Physical Drill & Arms Drill. Lt Col. G.S. BREWIS D.S.O. proceeded on leave to U.K. Lt. A.M. DICKINSON, U.S.R. M.C. att. 7 L.F. proceeded on leave to U.K.	
	27th		The Battn was inspected by the Divisional Commander & Medal Ribbons presented to the following Officers N.C.O.'s & others. Lt. W.F. O'BRYEN, Bar to M.C. Lt. H.E. WORDEN, The M.C., Sgt M. PINDER, L/Cpl PRINCE, D.C.M.'s, Sgt A. STRETCH, L/Cpl J. PICKERING, P/c T.W. MANNS, Pte J.H. BAILEY, M.M's, 2/Lt J.R. GARBUTT M.C. rejoined from leave from U.K.	
	28th		A & B Coys practised an attack scheme, C & D Coys training on the range. The Battn played the 42nd DIV R.E.'s at football in the Divisional Football Competition.	
	29th		The Battn had all their gas helmets tested. At D Coys practised an attack scheme. B & C Coys training in Physical Drill & Arms Drill. 2/Lt J.A. HADDOCK, 2/Lt M.M. UNSEY, 2/Lt G.H. UPTON, 2/Lt J.T. KITCHEN joined the Battn from England.	
	30th		The Battn went for a route march & round CADDRY.	
	31st		The Battn training in Tactical schemes, Assault schemes, Physical training & Lewis gun. MAJOR A.M.C. DEBENHAM rejoined from leave from U.K.	

Mess
Lt Col
Cdg 7th Bn Lan Fus.

31/10/18.

WAR DIARY

7th LANCASHIRE FUSILIERS

NOVEMBER 1918

VOL 52

WAR DIARY of 7/F Lancashire Fusiliers

or INTELLIGENCE SUMMARY.

Army Form C. 2118.

(Erase heading not required.)

Place	Date	Hour	Summary of Events and Information	Remarks and references to Appendices
FRANCE Sheet 57B 1-40000 Batt H.Q. at Itsal 61	Nov 1st		A & D Coys practised a combined attack & target scheme. B & C Coys Training on the range. Lewis gun classes & gas drill. A & B Coys at the Baths	MM
	2nd		The Battn. practised on attack scheme. Lewis gun classes, gas drill & Musketry. C Coy at the Baths	MM
	3rd		Church parade in the 1/5 L.F. lines. D Coy at the Baths.	
	4th		7th LAN FUS won the Combined Bugle & Brass Band Event in the DIVISIONAL BAND CONTEST.	MM
			Bn. marched to SOLESMES via BETHENCOURT, VIESLY & BRIASTE. 2/Lt F.B. Welt proceeded on leave U.K.	QBT
	5.		Bn. marched to BEAUDIGNIES.	QBT
	6.		HERBIGNIES	QBT
	7.		Through FORÊT de MORMAL to PETIT BAVAY.	QBT
	8.	9am	Bn. marched out at 06.00 to assembly position in P.33.A along the railway line	
			Bn. H.Q. at BOUSSIERES. A Coy captured 1st objective Bois de QUESNEY. S of HAUTMONT without opposition. 5.30 A.M. the D/L/2	QBT
			The final objective road in P.20.A. C. P.26.A was taken about 12:00 noon. 9th instant. artillery recoil of a flanking movement by "B" and "D" Coys. attacked	see XI

WAR DIARY
or
INTELLIGENCE SUMMARY.
(Erase heading not required.)

Army Form C. 2118.

Place	Date	Hour	Summary of Events and Information	Remarks and references to Appendices
FRANCE Sheet 57B 1/40000	8th (Contin)		Capt Kelly (D'Coy) was wounded in the afternoon during	
	9th		Prisoners Captured 1 Officer 21 O.Rs. Two British prisoners of war were released Booty Captured Two motor wagons and three ammunition trains (82 trucks) At 22.00 hours the Bn took over the sector held by the 1/10 Manchesters in addition to our own line. 4 O.R. killed & 17 wounded. Throughout operation Bn H.Q. moved to HAUTMONT.	QBY
	9th		The Bn took over the whole divisional line which was patrolled by A-B'Coy C+D Coys returned to billets at HAUTMONT	QBY QBY
	10th		The Bn formed an outpost line and took over the whole of the CORPS Front	
	11th		ARMISTICE Hostilities ceased at 11.00 hours. The Bn Buglers sounded the STAND FAST and NO PARADE in the square at HAUTMONT. Corps Cyclist Bn took over from the Bn & the companies returned to billets in HAUTMONT.	QBY
	12th		1 Cpl 3 O.Rs buried with military honours in the cemetery at HAUTMONT. Coys chiefly difference & cleaning up after being in the line 2/LT. E.R. PATRICK & 2/LT. W.R.S. BARNETT joined Batt from base, 2/LT ASHWORTH from Brigade Lt. J. TEMPEST D.C.M. evacuated to	QBY

Army Form C. 2118.

WAR DIARY
or
INTELLIGENCE SUMMARY.
(Erase heading not required.)

Instructions regarding War Diaries and Intelligence Summaries are contained in F. S. Regs., Part II. and the Staff Manual respectively. Title pages will be prepared in manuscript.

Place	Date	Hour	Summary of Events and Information	Remarks and references to Appendices
Map Ref. FRANCE Sheet 57 1/40000	Nov. 13th		Route marches under Coy. arrangements. L/T A.M. DICKINSON rejoined from leave.	AMJ
	14th		Musketry & close order drill carried out	AMJ
	15th		Training as above. Baths at HAUTMONT. 2/Lt WALFORD rejoined from Hospital. Strength O 39 OR 657	AMJ
	16th		" " " 2 GERMAN GUNS presented to 6 the Div. to the sign of HAUTMONT	
	17th		L/T H.M. GOULD M.C. to hospital. Notification received that D.S.O. had been awarded to L/T.Col. T.J. KELLY M.C. Church parade. Capt C.Y.G.B. R.J. SOMERVILLE rejoined for duty from ROUEN.	AMJ AMJ
	18th		Batt. rout marched FONTAINE – LIMONT FONTAINE – LE PAYE, L/T H. HOWE to T.A.R.M's dept. Div.	AMJ
	19th		Company Training.	AMJ
	20th		" 2 Batt. Ceremonial Drill	AMJ
	21st		" Baths for the whole Batt. Divisional Rugby Competition v 8th MANCHESTER Regt.	AMJ
			the Batt. won 6 points to 3	
	22nd		Batt. rout marched REMY MAL BATL – LIMONT FONTAINE – FONTAINE. Capt & Q.M. G.H. PAYNE 4F the Batt. to proceed to ABBEVILLE	AMJ
	23rd		Company training. No Batt. Drill. Lt P. YATES. 2/Lt L. ORR. 2/Lt R.W. HODGKINS joined from base.	AMJ AMJ
	24th		Church parade. Lt V.L. EVANS joined from base. Divl Rugby Comp v Coy R.E. Lost 3pts – 3	AMJ
	25th		Companies training in vicinity of WILLETS. Transport Competition. Officers Mess started	AMJ

Army Form C. 2118.

WAR DIARY
or
INTELLIGENCE SUMMARY.
(Erase heading not required.)

Instructions regarding War Diaries and Intelligence Summaries are contained in F. S. Regs., Part II. and the Staff Manual respectively. Title pages will be prepared in manuscript.

Place	Date	Hour	Summary of Events and Information	Remarks and references to Appendices
MAP REF. FRANCE Sheet 51 1/40000	Nov. 26th		Brigade Route March with Transport. P30 c 4.3 – LES GRAVETTES – LOUVROIL – ST LAZARE – Q9 Central – Fork Rds Q17 c 4.3 – FERRIERE – Q23 c 4.6 – T Roads Q 28 c 2.6 – Q14 Q13 Q26 c 3.3 – FORT D'HAUTMONT.	AW/ AW/
	27th		Company Training. Capt. P.E. BRIERLEY from course. Lt. F.B. WEBB from leave.	
	28th		Route March. Capt. B. SHELMERDINE from hospital. 2/Lt. H. MUNSEY from course. 2/Lt. S.S. WRIGHT from leave.	AW/
	29th		Company Training & Batt. Drill.	
	30th		Brigade Route March with Transport. FONTAINE – LIMONT FONTAINE – ECLAIBES – BEAUFORT OR FORT D'HAUTMONT. S.Times/A 44 – 706 D	AW/

Westby Wright
Maj.
Cg. 7th Lan. Fus.

Headquarters,
125th Brigade.

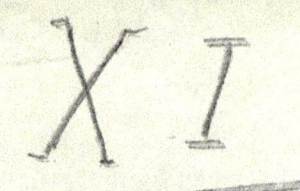

SUMMARY OF OPERATIONS.
November 4th to November 11th, 1918.

The Battalion left FONTAINE au PIRE after 12 days rest and marched on the 1st day to SOLESMES, 2nd day - BEAUDIGNIES, and 3rd day - HERBIGNIES. Here the 125th Brigade became Support Brigade to the Division, and orders were received to prepare to take over the line the following day, November 7th.

Leaving HERBIGNIES at 11 o'clock on the morning of the 7th November, the Battalion received orders to proceed to HARGNIES to billet, passing through the FORET DE MORMAL. The march through the forest was very difficult and exhausting owing to the bad state of the roads and the congestion of traffic, and in many cases it was necessary to unload limbers and make a portage round craters. At 3.p.m. it was learned that HARGNIES had only just been captured and that it was not possible to billet there, and orders were then received to proceed to PETIT BAVAY.

At 7.a.m. next morning the Battalion left billets and marched through PONT SUR SAMBRES and PANTIGNY to an assembly position West of the railway in P.33.a. and c. The 1/5th Lancashire Fusiliers on the right formed up in V.3.a. There was no touch with troops on the left, the general position being that the 126th Brigade held the North and North-East corner of HAUTMONT. There was no artillery barrage. The troops passed forward at 11.30.a.m. and A. Coy., captured the 1st objective running North and South through P.29.central. The advance was continued with C.Coy., on the left and B.Coy., on the right. The orders were to pass through the first objective in a North Easterly direction, swinging to the East at

FORT HAUTMONT in order to reach the final objective, the AVESNES - MAUBEUGE Road from Q.26.a.2.4. to Cross Roads Q.20.a.9.8. (LES GRAVETTES). There were no signs of the enemy until the troops attempted to debouch from the Eastern outskirts of HAUTMONT, whereupon heavy Machine Gun fire was opened from the direction of FORT HAUTMONT and the high ground North of it. Towards dusk this fire grew much less and small patrols were able to advance in the low country in P.24.b. and P.19.a.

At 9.p.m. further orders were given for C. Coy., to advance and outflank the enemy's position. This was done successfully and the final objective was reached by both C. and B. Coys., at about 3.30.a.m. on the 9th inst. 1 officer and 21 other ranks were captured. Scouts and fighting patrols were pushed out immediately and reached the villages of FERRIERE LE GRAND, LES TRIEUX and FERRIERE LE PETIT. Great quantities of booty were found in LES TRIEUX, including 3 ammunition trains.

At 9.a.m. on the 9th November, two troops of the 3rd Hussars passed through the Battalion. During the afternoon of the 9th, A. Coy., relieved C. and B. Coys., in final objective, taking over the whole Battalion front, and C. Coy., side-slipped and relieved the 1/5th Lancashire Fusiliers who held the line from Q.26.a.2.4. to LE PAYE and the remaining Coys., were withdrawn to billets at HAUTMONT. On the morning of the 10th further re-arrangements were made, the Battalion taking over the whole Corps front from LES GRAVETTES on the North to the Cross Roads, W.13 central. A. Coy. held from LES GRAVETTES to LE PAYE and C. Coy., from LE PAYE to W.13. central. B. Coy.

(3).

remained at HAUTMONT as in support to A. Coy., and B. Coy., proceeded to FONTAINE as in support to C. Coy.,   The general scheme was to establish examining posts on the road to stop unauthorised civilian traffic, as by this time the Cavalry and Cyclists had passed through and the enemy had gone back several miles.

After the armistice came into operation on November 11th the Battalion was relieved by the IV Corps Cyclist Battalion and all Coys., returned to billets in HAUTMONT.

The casualties during the operations were :-

    1 Officer   -   Wounded.
    4 O.Rs.   -   Killed.
    17 O.Rs.   -   Wounded.

2/12/18.

Lieut. Colonel,
Commanding 7th Lancashire Fusiliers.

WAR DIARY.

7th LANCASHIRE FUSILIERS.

DECEMBER. 1918.

VOL. 53.

WAR DIARY of 7TH LAN. FUS.

INTELLIGENCE SUMMARY

Army Form C. 2118.

Place	Date	Hour	Summary of Events and Information	Remarks and references to Appendices
Map Ref. FRANCE 51 1/40,000	Dec. 1918 1st		Voluntary Batt. parade to line the MAUBEUGE–AVESNES Road on the occasion of H.M. The KING passing by.	
	2nd		Company training	
	3rd		Batt. Route march	
	4th		Company training. Advanced Guard Exc. W of Rly. for CHARLEROI	
	5th		Bnd. Route march	
	6th		Company training - by teams in reading, writing & arithmetic. Class going under LT. A.F. WORDEN M.C.	
	7th		L/C for ENGLAND to bring back Rgt. Colours.	
	8th		Company Training - inspection of billeting area by C.O.	
	9th		Church parade. A party of 1 Officer & 25 O.Rs. left to take over as Guard over looted German War material at ST. GERVAIS. CAPT. AW. AMOND proceeded to join 2nd YORK & LANCS NAMUR	
	10th		Company Training. Battalion drill, Physical training & Squad Drill. CAPT. R.B. BREWIS M.C.	
	11th		Proceeded to CHARLEROI.	
			Brigade Route march.	
	12th		Company training in Musketry, Close order drill, Battalion drill	

Army Form C. 2118.

WAR DIARY OF 7th LAN FUS,
or
INTELLIGENCE SUMMARY.
(Erase heading not required.)

Instructions regarding War Diaries and Intelligence Summaries are contained in F. S. Regs., Part II. and the Staff Manual respectively. Title pages will be prepared in manuscript.

Place	Date	Hour	Summary of Events and Information	Remarks and references to Appendices
FRANCE Nov. 1 - 10.000.0	13th		The Battn preparing for the move. Capt. B.E. Brierley proceeded on leave to U.K.	JWM
	14th		The Battn marched from HAUTMONT to MAUBEUGE & billetted there for the night. CAPT. W.F. O'BRYEN M.C. awarded a second bar to his M.C. LIEUT. F.B. WEBB and 2/LT J.M. McCREADY awarded the M.C.	JWM
Nord. Belgium 1-100000	15th		The Battn marched from MAUBEUGE to ESTINNE-au-MONT, via BERSILLES - VILLERS-SIRE-NICOLE - TRIEUX & billetted there for the night	JWM
	16th		The Battn marched from ESTINNE-au-MONT to ANDERLIES, via BINCHE & billetted there for two nights	JWM
	17th		The day spent in cleaning up & preparing for the final march to CHARLEROI.	JWM
	18th		The Battn marched from ANDERLIES to CHARLEROI.	JWM
	19		The day spent in cleaning out the barracks. LIEUT A.E. WORDEN M.C. & party returned from ENGLAND with the Colours.	JWM
	20th		The day spent in cleaning out the barracks	JWM
	21st		O.C. Coys moved to the Cavalry Barracks. 2/LT. J.M. McCREADY M.C. proceeded on leave to U.K.	JWM

Army Form C. 2118.

WAR DIARY of 7th LAM FUS.
or
INTELLIGENCE SUMMARY.
(Erase heading not required.)

Instructions regarding War Diaries and Intelligence Summaries are contained in F. S. Regs., Part II. and the Staff Manual respectively. Title pages will be prepared in manuscript.

Place	Date	Hour	Summary of Events and Information	Remarks and references to Appendices
France Auth/HMM	22nd		Church parade. The Batt'n had a lecture on AMERICA	MM
	23rd		Coys training in arms Drill, Close Order Drill. 22 O.R's proceeded to Concentration Camp for Demobilization	MM
	24		Battalion parade. Coys training in Physical Training & Close Order Drill. Lectures	
			2/LT. J.E. ASHWORTH M.C. proceeded on leave to U.K. LT. A.F. WORDEN M.C.	MM
			100 O.R's proceeded to the Concentration Camp for Demobilization	
	25th		Church parade. The Divisional Commander inspected the training Halls. 2 O.R.s	MM
			proceeded to Concentration Camp for Demobilization	MM
	26th		Recreational Training. 7 O.R's proceeded to the Concentration Camp for Demobilization	MM
	27th		Working parties.	MM
	28th		Company training in Physical Training & Close Order Drill	MM
	29th		Church parade.	MM
	30th		Working parties. A & C Coys at the Baths. Company training in Close Order Drill	MM
	31st		Educational Training, Working parties. D Coy at the Baths	MM

[signature]
Lieut Colonel
Cdg. 7 = Lancashire Fusiliers

Headquarters.
125 Bde.

42

Herewith War Diary for
the month of January. 1919

1.2.19

J.B.Well Lieut
for Lieut. Colonel.
Commdg 7th Lan. Fus.

WAR DIARY of 7th AM. F.O.S.

or

INTELLIGENCE SUMMARY.

(Erase heading not required.)

Army Form C. 2118.

Vol 24

Place	Date	Hour	Summary of Events and Information	Remarks and references to Appendices
FRANCE	Jan 1st		Company training in Close book drill & Physical training. Battalion dined	1/W
MAMUA	2nd		Working parties. Educational Classes. Physical Training	2/W
T-IOT DO	3rd		Brigade Route march. MAJOR LEDEF proceeded on leave to U.K.	4/W
	4th		Educational Classes. Company training in Close Order drill & Physical Training	5/W
	5th		Church parades	6/W
	6th		Company Training in Close Order drill & Physical Training. Musketry Kit inspection	7/W
	7th		Educational Classes. Working parties	8/W
	8th		Company training in Close Order drill, Physical Training & Lewis Gun training	9/W
			Working parties	
	9th		Educational Classes. A & B Coys at the Butts. Company training in Close Order drill	10/W
	10th		Company training. C & D Coys at the Butts. 2 LT. S.M. McCREADY 9 M.G. rejoined from	11/W
			leave. LIEUT R.D. THORP proceeded on leave to U.K.	
	11th		Educational Classes. Working parties	12/W
	12th		Church parades	13/W
	13th		Company training in Musketry, Close Order drill & Physical training. C Company	14/W
			on the range	

WAR DIARY of 7th LAN F US
or
INTELLIGENCE SUMMARY.

Army Form C. 2178.

(Erase heading not required.)

Place	Date	Hour	Summary of Events and Information	Remarks and references to Appendices
France	Jan.			
Hust	14th		Educational Classes, Physical Training, Working Parties	W.M
Namur	15th		Company Training, Kit Inspection, LIEUT E.W. CHASTNEY left the battalion for demobilisation	W.M
Montsin	16th		Educational Classes, Physical training A B & D Coys at the butts	W.M
	17th		Company training in Close Order drill, Musketry & Physical training, Lecture on South Africa	W.M
	18th		Divisional Commanders inspection & pollow presentation, Lecture on Demobilisation	W.M
	19th		Church Parade, CAPT F.W. COLLEY left the Battn for demobilisation	W.M
	20th		Company Training, Working parties, Lecture on the Navy	W.M
	21st		Educational Classes, Preparing for the G.O.C's inspection.	W.M
	22nd		Inspection by the G.O.C. Commanding 125 Brigade	W.M
	23rd		Educational Classes, Working parties, A Guard of 2 Officers & 23 O.R's proceeded to MONTIGNIES REGULATING STATION.	W.M
	24th		Company Training on the range, Working parties.	W.M
	25th		Educational Classes, Working parties	W.M
	26th		Church parade, 2/LIEUT. W.G. BROWN, proceeded on leave to U.K. 2/LT. W. PROCTER left the battalion for demobilisation	W.M

WAR DIARY of 7th LAN. FUS.
INTELLIGENCE SUMMARY

Army Form C. 2118.

Place	Date	Hour	Summary of Events and Information	Remarks and references to Appendices
FRANCE	JAN			
Henin	27th		Working parties. 2/LIEUT F.L. WALFORD, left the battalion for demobilisation	MMP
Henin t-Hortin	28th		Working parties. MAJOR. A/MAG. DEBENHAM. M.C. left the battalion for demobilisation	MMP
			LT.COL. G.S. BREWIS D.S.O. rejoined the battalion from England.	MMP
	29th		Working parties, LIEUT. G.D THORP, rejoined from leave	MMP
	30th		LT.COL. G.S. BREWIS D.S.O. took over command of the Battalion. LT.COL T.I.	MMP
			KELLY. D.S.O. M.C. proceeded on leave to U.K	MMP
	31st		Preparing for the move to MARCHIENNES-AU-PONT. Guard of 2 Officers & 77 O.R.s	MMP
			rejoined from MONTIGNIES.	

R.M. Nall
Major
for Lt. Colonel
Cdg 7th Lancashire Fusiliers

WAR DIARY of 4th Lancashire Fusiliers
or
INTELLIGENCE SUMMARY.

(Erase heading not required.)

Army Form C. 2118.

Vol 25

Place	Date	Hour	Summary of Events and Information	Remarks and references to Appendices
France Belgium Sheet NAMUR 1-100,000	Feb 1st		The Battalion moved from CHARLEROI to MARCHIENNE-AU-PONT to take over the IV Corps Concentration Camp.	HM
	2nd		Arranging billets	HM
	3rd		Working parties	HM
	4th		Company training in Close Order drill, Physical Training & Arms drill. CAPT. F.H. WILLIAMSON, proceeded on leave to U.K.	HM
	5th		Making arrangements for taking over the IV Corps Concentration Camp. MAJOR F. HORSFALL, M.C. proceeded for Demobilization.	HM
	6th		Preparing to take over the Concentration Camp.	HM
	7th		Company training in Close Order drill, Arms drill & Physical Training	HM
	8th		Educational Classes & Company training in Arms drill & Close Order drill	HM
	9th		Church parade, LIEUT P YATES proceeded to 16th LAN.FUS Concentration Camp for demobilization. Ordered to send a draft to 16th LAN.FUS of 8 Officers & 140 O.R.s	HM
	10th		Educational classes. Prepare the draft for the 16th LAN. FUS	HM
	11th		Company training in Close Order drill, Arms drill & Physical training	HM
	12th		Took over two Coys at the IV Corps Concentration Camp.	HM

Army Form C. 2118.

WAR DIARY of 7th Lancashire Fusiliers
or
INTELLIGENCE SUMMARY.
(Erase heading not required.)

Instructions regarding War Diaries and Intelligence Summaries are contained in F. S. Regs., Part II. and the Staff Manual respectively. Title pages will be prepared in manuscript.

Place	Date	Hour	Summary of Events and Information	Remarks and references to Appendices
Belgium Nr of NAMUR	Feb 13th		Company training in Close order drill, Arms drill & Physical Training	
1-10-000	14th		Company training in Arms drill, Physical Training & Musketry, on inspection of the Draft.	
	15th		Company training in Bayonet fighting, Close order drill & Arms drill. LIEUT. D.G. McLACHLAN proceeded to IV Corps Concentration Camp for demonstration.	
	16th		2/LIEUT. W.G. BROWN rejoined from leave. Church parade.	
	17th		Company training in Musketry, Bayonet fighting & Close order drill.	
			CAPT. R.J. SOMERVILLE proceeded on leave to U.K.	
	18th		Company training in Arms drill, Close order drill & Physical Training. LIEUT. COLONEL G.S. BREW'S DSO took over command of the IV Corps Concentration Camp. CAPT. W.J. O'BRYEN MC rejoined from leave.	
	19th		Company training in Close order drill, Arms drill & Bayonet fighting	
	20th		Company training in Musketry, Close order drill & Physical Training	
	21st		Company training in Arms drill, Physical Training & Musketry. CAPT. F.H. WILLIAMSON rejoined from leave	

WAR DIARY of 7th Lancashire Fusiliers.

INTELLIGENCE SUMMARY.

Army Form C. 2118.

(Erase heading not required.)

Place	Date	Hour	Summary of Events and Information	Remarks and references to Appendices
Belgium				
About	22nd		Company Training in Close Order drill, Arms drill & Musketry	
	23rd		Church Parades	
NAMUR	24th		Company Training in Musketry, Bayonet fighting & Physical Training	
m/Meuse			MAJOR. C. ALDERSON. D.S.O. proceeded on leave to U.K.	
	25th		Bn. left went for a Route March	
	26th		Company Training in Close Order drill, Arms drill & Physical Training	
	27th		Company Training in Musketry, Bayonet fighting & Physical Training	
	28th		Company Training in Arms drill, Close Order drill & Physical Training	

G.S. Bravin, Lieut Colonel
Cdg 7th Lancashire Fusiliers

CONFIDENTIAL.

Vol 26

H5.L.
4 sheets

WAR
DIARY
Vol. 56.

1/7 Batt. Lan. Fus.

1st – 31st March. 1919.

Army Form C. 2118.

WAR DIARY of 7th Lancashire Fusiliers
or
INTELLIGENCE SUMMARY.

(Erase heading not required.)

Instructions regarding War Diaries and Intelligence Summaries are contained in F. S. Regs., Part II. and the Staff Manual respectively. Title pages will be prepared in manuscript.

Place	Date	Hour	Summary of Events and Information	Remarks and references to Appendices
Belgium Sheet NAMUR 1	March 1st		Company Training in Musketry, Bayonet fighting & Physical Training	
1-100000	2nd		Church Parades	
	3rd		Company Training in Close order drill, Arms drill & Physical Training.	
	4th		Company Training in Musketry, Arms drill & Physical Training. C.Q.M.S. W. FINN 241775 SGT R.C. JOHNSON and 28/161 SGT J. PICKUP awarded the MILITARY MEDAL	
	5th		Company Training in Close Order drill, Arms drill & Physical Training	
	6th		Company Training in Musketry, Bayonet fighting & Physical Training	
	7th		Company Training in Musketry & Arms drill – Rugby Tourney	
	8th		Company Training in Close Order drill – Physical Training & Bayonet fighting	
	9th		Church Parade	
	10th		Company Training in Physical Training, Musketry, Close order drill	
	11th		Sgt. G.H. UPTON (M.M.) proceeded on leave to U.K. (on Leave 12/3/19)	
	12th		Company Training in Physical Training, Arms drill, & Close Order drill	
	13th		Company Training in Physical Training, Musketry & Bayonet fighting Draft Completion on March Discipline & Full Marching order	

WAR DIARY of 7th Lancashire Fusiliers

INTELLIGENCE SUMMARY.
(Erase heading not required.)

Army Form C. 2118.

Place	Date	Hour	Summary of Events and Information	Remarks and references to Appendices
Belgium Huts	March 14th		Company Training in Close Order Drill, Arms Drill & Physical Training	MM
NAMUR	15th		MAJOR C. ALDERSON D.S.O. rejoined from leave from U.K. Company Training in Close Order Drill & Arms Drill, Platoon Football Competition. CAPT. P.E. BRIERLEY proceeded to the 15th LANCASHIRE FUSILIERS	MM
1-100000	16th		Church Parade	MM
	17th		Company Training in Close Order Drill, Platoon Football Competition. 2/LIEUT J.T. Kitchen proceeded on leave to U.K.	MM
	18th		Company Training in Arms Drill, Close Order Drill & Physical Training. Bn West Interpretation Competition. LIEUT. J.M. CLIMIE rejoined from leave	MM
	19th			MM
	20th		Company Training in Arms Drill, Close Order Drill & Physical Training the Battalion at the Baths at Chedevie. 2/LIEUT J.R. GAIRBUTT M.S.	MM
	21st		proceeded on leave to U.K.	MM
	22nd		Company Training in Arms Drill, Close Order Drill & Guard Mounting	MM
	23rd		Church Parade	MM
	24th		Draft Competition in Full Marching Order & Guard Mounting	MM
	25th		Company Training in Arms Drill & Close Order Drill	MM

WAR DIARY of 7TH LANCASHIRE FUSILIERS. Army Form C. 2118.

or

INTELLIGENCE SUMMARY.

(Erase heading not required.)

Place	Date	Hour	Summary of Events and Information	Remarks and references to Appendices
BELGIUM SHEET NAMUR 1=100,000	March 26th		Inspection of draft. Company training in Arms Drill and Squad Drill.	109B
	27th		Lieut. H. Howe proceeded to H.Q. Chinese Labour Corps November. Billet inspection. Company training in Squad Drill and Arms Drill	109B
	28th		Billet inspection. Company training in Squad Drill and Arms Drill	109B 109B
	29th		Lieut. J.M. Climie attached to 9th Lancashire Fusiliers. Inspection of draft. Tug-of-war competition.	109B 109B
	30th		The following proceeded to 4th Concentration Camp for demobilisation. Major C. Alderson DSO, Lieut. J. McCready MC, Lieut H.M. Gould MC, 2/Lieut W.R.S. Barnett, and 2/Lieut S.S. Wright.	109B
	31st		Inspection of draft. Company training — Squad Drill and Arms drill.	109B
	30th		Competition. Inspection of Cadre by Commanding Officer. Lt Col. C.S. Brown DSO. took over 125 Bde Orders.	

G.S. Brown. Lt Col.
Cmdg 7th Lancashire Fusiliers

42
24 Cancel
Vol 27

WAR DIARY
OF
INTELLIGENCE SUMMARY.
(Erase heading not required.)

Army Form C. 2118.

of 7th Lancashire Fusiliers

46.C
1 sheet

Place	Date	Hour	Summary of Events and Information	Remarks and references to Appendices
Belgium Sheet 1	April 1st		2/LIEUT R.W. HODGKINS, 2/LIEUT E.R. PATRICK + 98 O.R.s proceeded to Hd.	////
NAMUR	2nd		16th Bn LAN. FUS.	////
1–10000			The Cadre preparing to go to England	////
	3rd		2/LIEUT J.T. KITCHEN received from there	////
	4th		2/LIEUT J.T. KITCHEN proceeded to 16th Bn LAN. FUS.	////
	5th		Checking all the Cadre stores	////
	6th		Church parades.	////
	7th		The Commanding Officer inspected the Cadre	////
	8th		The Cadre training in Arms drill. CAPT. F.H. WILLIAMSON proceeded to	////
			ENGLAND for demobilization.	////
	9th		The Cadre training in Arms drill. CAPT. E.C. SINGTON proceeded to	////
			ENGLAND for demobilization.	////
	10th		Preparing for the move to ANTWERP	////
	11th		Packing up stores loading limbers	////

G.S. Brown, Lieut Colonel
Cmdg 7 Lancashire Fusiliers

www.ingramcontent.com/pod-product-compliance
Lightning Source LLC
Chambersburg PA
CBHW081540160426
43191CB00011B/1802